Between Water and Song:
New Poets for the Twenty-First Century

Between Water and Song

New Poets for the Twenty-First Century

Edited by
Norman Minnick

WHITE PINE PRESS / BUFFALO, NEW YORK

ACKNOWLEDGMENTS begin on page 307.

The publication of this book has been made possible with public funds from the New York State Council on the Arts, a State Agency.

First Edition

Library of Congress Control Number: 2009932984

ISBN: 978-1-935210-07-8

Printed and bound in the United States of America

Cover photograph: Waterfall, Big Sur by Dennis Maloney

White Pine Press
P.O. Box 236
Buffalo, NY 14201

www.whitepine.org

Contents

Jay Leeming

Terrance Hayes

Eugene Gloria

Brian Turner

Joshua Poteat

Maurice Manning

Chris Abani

THE DEEP PULSE OF THE SPIRIT:
THE NEED FOR DEPTH AT THE BEGINNING
OF THE TWENTY-FIRST CENTURY

These two depths: the vertical holds the zenith and the
nadir; the other, this one, the horizontal, stretches to the
four unboundaries.

—Juan Ramón Jiménez

Now I a fourfold vision see,
And a fourfold vision is given to me.

—William Blake

In William Blake's *The Four Zoas,* the primal man, Albion, represents
Man before the Fall, and/or each of us in a state of sleep or unawak-
ened consciousness. In such a state the four fundamental aspects of
man have been thrown off balance. These are represented in Blake's
cosmology by the Four Zoas: Urizen, *rationality;* Luvah, *emotion;*
Tharmas, *sensation;* and Urthona, *intuition* or *imagination.* Jim Watt tells

us, "Though they are present in each of us, they are also uniquely and individually unbalanced—and a considerable effort is required to bring them into balance." He continues, "The Zoas... will assist us in that recovery and recreation of one another and reality which Blake calls the building of Jerusalem." In that process, I would say we begin to acknowledge vertical energy and allow the depths to open, transforming the flatness of mundane reality into genuine profundity and opening ourselves to a more soulful, more spiritual existence. Then we will no longer be dealing with exhausted elements of the horizontal, that energy-less vacuum in which we find ourselves, and in which "most American poets resemble blind men moving gingerly along the ground from tree to tree, from house to house, feeling each thing for a long time, and then calling out 'House!' when we already know it is a house." This is Robert Bly, who, along with Roberto Juarroz, is the greatest proponent of vertical energy in poetry. The vertical then is perhaps best characterized by example, just as Lorca's *duende* is best described as "a struggle, not a thought." Albanian poet Luljeta Lleshanaku's "The Bed" is such an example. It begins,

> My bed, a temple
> where murmurs of a stifled prayer press
> against my palate.
>
> Frozen genitalia
> buried fruit, imperfect fruit
> clean green leaves stretching out beneath the blankets
>
> to reach you, your warmth
> dew on the skin of a morning dream.

As she leaps from the image of the bed as temple to the buried, imperfect fruit of genitalia, to the skin of a morning dream, we are jarred from sleep and for a moment discover the sacredness of the world we live in. In other words, where we truly are.

Jung adopted these four elements of the horizontal and vertical realms as the four basic psychological functions by which we apprehend and evaluate our experiences. Marie-Louise von Franz, discussing these four functions in her *Interpretation of Fairy Tales*, says, "The more you have developed and obtained the use of more conscious functions, the better and the more colorful your interpretation will be." She continues, "It is an *art* which has to be practiced (italics mine)." Now, at the dawn of a new century, too many young people are sleepwalking and are oblivious to the world around them. We are desperate for poetry that is alive and wild, but at the same time provides us something to hold on to which we have only halfway accomplished with horizontal thought.

A graduate student in a creative writing program said recently that we shouldn't read anyone before the previous generation of poets because their poems don't include cell phones and iPods and thus have nothing to say to the modern poet. Many young poets are looking only to the poets of their own generation or teachers in their respective MFA programs, rather than, say, Li Po, Sappho, Mistral, or Machado. We are experiencing what I call "American Idol Syndrome." An aspiring singer tells the audience that her influences include Mariah Carey, Pink, or Hannah Montana rather than Billie Holiday, Bessie Smith, or Kirsten Flagstad. I am reminded of what Denise Levertov says in her essay "Great Possessions,"

> Much of what is currently acclaimed, in poetry as well as in prose, does not go beyond the most devitalized ordinary speech. Like the bleached dead wheat of which so much American bread is made (supposedly "enriched" by returning to the worthless flour a small fraction of the life that was once in it) such poems bloat us but do not nourish.

What's ignored is a deeper connection with the inner, or spiritual, life. Too many poets stay on the dry surface while volleying back and forth between the *rational* and the *emotional.* They do not honor the vertical energy that is necessary for a deeper, more soulful and spiritual life experience. Vertical awareness, then, must include *sensation* and *intuition* or *imagination,* "a movement down," as Bly says, "into earthly body, dirt, appetite, gross desire, death; and a movement toward sunlight, time, fulfillment, lily blossoms, purity, narcissus flowers, beauty, opening...." There is a desperate need for vertical awareness in poetry today. Our culture has become flatter and more superficial and horizontal than ever before.

But we must be careful and not think that we can exist solely in the vertical realm. Good poets are careful not to hastily leave the earth or the body; they resist effortless transcendence where New Age abstractions and thoughts of bliss and harmony result in egotistical self-absorption. Kevin Goodan, who was raised in Montana, fought forest fires for many years and lived on a farm in western Massachusetts, is very close to the soil, potato plants, thistles, fresh dung, and the earthly body. He says, "The Lord is a place / to dig down into" ("August"). Goodan is an expert at vertical awareness. He is always listening, paying attention, to the world around him, which may be all we are asked to do. In "Theories of Implication" he notes, "It begins in the leaves, / a hush that precedes all weather."

Maurice Manning, from Kentucky, also meditates on God, but here through the voice of Daniel Boone. Notice his attention to things of the natural world. Here he considers a god "who lives in the shadow / between two rocks and sleeps on moss, content / with the smallness of his task; the god who bends / rivers, the god who flecks the breast of a hawk..." ("On God"). His third collection *Bucolics,* a collection of psalms, or as the book jacket declares, "love songs to creation," is about as close to the mystical experience as a contemporary poet could hope to get. But notice how he doesn't simply give in to transcendence. Notice how he seeks it through soil and flesh. Notice the detail. Notice how he addresses God.

When I first started thinking about these ideas I wanted to use the term spiritual, but was afraid that it would leave out the depths of the soul and conjure up religious or new-agey abstractions. So I turned to two of my spiritual fathers, Antonio Machado and Rainer Maria Rilke. Machado says, "The substance of poetry does not lie in the sound value of the word, nor in its color, nor in the metric line, nor in the complex sensations, but in the deep pulse of the spirit…." It is in this manner I wish to use the term. For me, depth of spirit is the substance of poetry and is not an optional or decorative item like rhyme or assonance. In this way poetry is alive, organic, pulsing. "How many readers today, how many poets, consider poetry as a spiritual practice?" Stephen Mitchell asks in his introduction to Rilke's *Sonnets to Orpheus*, "But when we take it seriously enough, the poem becomes transparent, becomes the world illuminated." Rilke says in *Letters to a Young Poet*, "Go into yourself. Find out the reason that commands you to write; see whether it has spread its roots into the very depths of your heart; confess to yourself whether you would have to die if you were forbidden to write." He also says, "A work of art is good if it has risen out of necessity."

Are poets necessary? Joseph Campbell says, "Artists share the calling, according to their disciplines and crafts, to cast the new images of mythology. That is, they provide the contemporary metaphors that allow us to realize the transcendent, infinite, and abundant nature of being as it is." Poets who resist the "deep pulse of the spirit" will cast images that do the opposite. Their poems will provide scant metaphors, if they provide any at all. Muriel Rukeyser warns, "If we do not go deep, if we live and write halfway, there are obscurity, vulgarity, the slang of fashion, and several kinds of death."

We need substance—poetry that will acknowledge the things of this world and the space between things. Here is the opening of Joshua Poteat's "Documenting the Birds: Office Park" from his collection *Ornithologies*:

> If this is what we become
> > then let me turn into light now while the spaces
> between the leaves have enough room to hold me.

If we acknowledge the soul, poetry will arouse the bottom-dwelling creatures we have suppressed with rational thought. Maria Melendez has a message for the horizontal thinker:

> Know this, all humanists:
>
> under the pure, lifeless
> surface of the Sea
> of Thought swims a great
>
> gray whale, scarred
> and barnacled, carrying
> a calf, a great gray whale
>
> about to breach.

Melendez isn't about to suggest that what comes from the depths is going to be pretty. We are not entering safe territory. It is the darkness we must descend into before attaining the spiritual. The term spirituality should not be thought of as a method of escape from earthly life. We need to make a clear distinction between spirit and soul. Poets who exist only in the vertical realm are as imbalanced as those on the horizontal plane; most are treading furiously to keep their heads in the spiritual realm and tend to avoid the depths of the soul.

Melendez understands the danger of trying to stay only in the vertical realm. She knows that Campbell's mandate is necessary but that it is a heavy load to carry. If we are willing to go into the depths we must have something—myth, ritual—to keep the energy contained. Melendez would agree with Ted Hughes:

> When wise men know how to create rituals and dogma, the energy can be contained. When the old rituals and dogma lost credit and disintegrated, and no new ones have been formed, the energy cannot be contained, and so its effect is destructive…. That is why force of any

kind frightens our rationalist, humanist style of out-look.... If you refuse the energy, you are living a kind of death. If you accept the energy, it destroys you. What is the alternative? To accept the energy, and find methods of turning it to good, of keeping it under con-trol—rituals, the machinery of religion.

I don't want to pigeonhole poetry into a category or school of thought. I fear that this introduction is already starting to sound too technical, lacking the energy it portrays. It is starting to sound like tenets of "The New Sincerity," which emphasizes human connection over the irony, disconnection and lofty cynicism of postmodernism. Although sincerity isn't a bad idea, "The New Sincerity" is a "school" of thought, which is why I welcome any throwing off of a system. The Trickster is always trotting around the edge of town ready to do that. Sherwin Bitsui is a young poet from White Cone, Arizona. He is Diné of the Bitter Water People, born for the Manygoats People. Trickster energy runs throughout his poems. He says of the Trickster,

> He was there—
> before the rising action rose to meet this acre cornered by
>   thirst,
> before birds swallowed bathwater and exploded in
>   midsentence,
> before the nameless
> began sipping the blood of ravens from the sun's knotted
>   atlas.

When Trickster energy is not allowed to enter we fall into banality and apathy. Lewis Hyde tells us, "The road that trickster travels is a spirit road as well as a road in fact. He is the adept who can move between heaven and earth, and between the living and the dead." This is vertical awareness.

Reinvigorated in recent issues of *Poetry* and *American Poetry Review** is the age-old polarity that claims poetry should either be horizontal or vertical. But as we have seen, the result of polar opposites can only be tension, unless there is a unifying element. This is where the artist comes in. "All writers should be obliged to scrutinize the idiots of both persuasions, left and right," Adam Zagajewski, one of our greatest advocates for ardor, real soul in the arts and the spiritual life, says, "The poet is a born centrist; his parliament is elsewhere." So if we begin to apprehend this vertical energy we will be doing poetry's true work, writing from this "parliament of elsewhere," leaving the flatness for a more genuine and dynamic life of the soul. In an earlier essay Zagajewski suggests, "Poetic imagination creates rather than comes to know reality." The artist must ask, What sort of reality are we creating?

The severe drought caused by Language poetry and the tedium and irony of the postmodernists are certainly contributing to the ruin. My father went into a bookstore and asked for a recommendation. The salesperson handed him a book by a young, "up-and-coming" poet. My father, one of the most well read people I know, said that he simply couldn't figure out what she was talking about in her poems. Neither could I. He said he got the feeling he wasn't welcome into "the club." What is in these poems for the reader? Who should poems be written for anyway? Pablo Neruda says, "Poetry has lost its ties with the reader... It has to get him back... It has to walk in the darkness and encounter the heart of man, the eyes of woman, the stranger in the street, those who at twilight or in the middle of the starry night feel the need for at least one line of poetry."

The idea of this anthology is not to be all-inclusive. We felt that the reader would get a better idea of the poet's body of work if we were to include more poems than are typically found in an anthology. Each of these poets was born after 1960 (young by poet standards). They are simply the most intriguing poets writing today. I am especially indebted to Valzhyna Mort and Mira Rosenthal for their countless hours discussing and arguing the merits of such poetry, especially in the earlier stages of this project, and to Robert Bly,

Alison Granucci, Jane Hirshfield, Mary Karr, Dennis Maloney, Katie Rauk, David Shumate, Jim Watt, and Adam Zagajewski and their unflagging support for this project.

*I have in mind essays by Tony Hoagland [*Fear of Narrative and the Skittery Poem of Our Moment* (March 2006)] and John Barr [*American Poetry in the New Century* (September 2006)] in *Poetry* and Dana Levin [*The Heroics of Style: A Study in Three Parts, Part Three* (March/April 2006)] in *APR* and the letters in response to those essays.

Works Cited

Bitsui, Sherwin. *Shapeshift.* Tucson: U of Arizona, 2003.

Bly, Robert. *Neruda & Vallejo: Selected Poems.* Beacon, 1993.

Campbell, Joseph. *Thou Art That.* Novato: New World Library, 2001.

Faas, Ekbert. *Ted Hughes: The Unaccommodated Universe.* Santa Barbara: Black Sparrow, 1980.

Forman, Ruth. *Renaissance.* Boston: Beacon, 1997.

Goodan, Kevin. *In the Ghost-House Acquainted.* Farmington: Alice James, 2004.

Hyde, Lewis. *Trickster Makes This World.* New York: North Point, 1998.

Levertov, Denise. *New & Selected Essays.* New York: New Directions, 1992.

Lleshanaku, Luljeta. *Fresco.* New York: New Directions, 2002.

Machado, Antonio. *Times Alone.* Trans. Robert Bly. Hanover: Wesleyan UP, 1983.

Manning, Maurice. *A Companion for Owls.* Orlando: Harcourt, 2004.

Melendez, Maria. *How Long She'll Last in This World.* Tucson: U of Arizona, 2006.

Nelson, Howard. *On the Poetry of Galway Kinnell: The Wages of Dying.* Ann Arbor: U of Michigan, 1987.

Neruda, Pablo. *Memoirs.* Trans. Hardie St. Martin. New York: Penguin, 1974.

Poteat, Joshua. *Ornithologies.* Tallahassee: Anhinga, 2006.

Rilke, Rainer Maria. *The Sonnets to Orpheus.* Trans. Stephen Mitchell, New York, Touchstone, 1985.

—. *Letters to a Young Poet,* Trans. Stephen Mitchell. New York: Random House, 1984.

Rukeyser, Muriel. *The Life of Poetry.* Ashfield: Paris P, 1996.

Watt, Jim. *Work Toward Knowing: Beginning with Blake.* Unpublished.

Zagajewski, Adam. *Another Beauty.* Athens: U. of Georgia, 2002.

—. *Solidarity, Solitude.* New York: Ecco, 1990.

Ruth Forman

If any poet best embodies the energy that passes between soul and spirit, water and song, it is Ruth Forman. She moves with grace, sincerity and a fierceness I haven't seen in a long time. From hymns to haiku her poems possess the freshness, vitality and truth of old stories that have been passed down from generation to generation. "Speak what you know without translation," she says, "like your spirit already knows."

If You Write Poetry

Go to the ground

it should make the ancestors put down their pipes
and let you tell the story
it should make the grandmothers rock
themselves like they rocked you
it should make your momma wonder
who you are
and your daddy feel
he's someplace real
like the root of your hair
and where you come from

Graduate School

The book not so big
for you to get lost in the pages
perhaps you don't find yourself in them
cause they so thin
and you so thick like buckwheat honey

trust your footsteps
trust your eyes and tongue

start easy
one or two sentences per class
feel comfortable with the sound of your voice
in a small room ten people one large table

speak your heart they will hear
hearts speak to each other
even when minds don't listen
walk with your neck showing

and when afraid

trust your footsteps
trust your eyes and tongue
they come from a long place long time

if you can't find
the root in your spine
stand still and wait with your hand on a wall
listen to its negotiations with gravity

until you find the lava flow solid from your veins

harden your back
rise your throat and over

then
speak what you know without translation
stand without negotiation
and fight

like your spirit already knows

Stand

why so afraid to stand up?
someone will tell you
sit down?

but here is the truth
someone will always tell you
sit down

the ones we remember
kept standing

Koi

have you seen a woman collapse have you
seen her bones melt while she grasps
a glass of white wine remembering have you
forced yourself not to look away

not easy
to hold up a grieving woman she falls through your fingers
like ashes of a husband passed seven weeks ago

have you felt tears weave the air from her fine piano have you
felt yourself crack

you still dare walk these halls
this oak floor bare foot

what gives you the right to open the refrigerator
find enough for a salad among celery going bad you

climb into her bed empty though you in it who are you

to uphold this house struggling death and life who are you

to hold her on your right shoulder pat her
into shape prayers and song for leavening

tell her she does good kiss her cheek when she lets you
touch her head when she's not busy
outrunning her heart, garden hose and laundry basket

maybe it's enough to bear witness with ivory candles
to a woman risen and fallen by love

still enough magic in her right hand to chase life
into a gold Koi you find gasping

on the ground she places him in water
coaxes his body
clockwise til he swims

with all fins

For Christine

Hand Me Your Palm

i trace a language
fingers touch skin slowly
wander your streams

somethin special bout hands
God gave them for more than picking things up
carved them to remind us
we have a long way to go

travelers we are
who've forgotten our packs
stop to build on the first dust heap we find
fill it with rock and wood and glass
breath a spirit through once in a while

traveler
what if we were to pack ourselves only
and continue downstream
leave the wood and her sisters behind
what would we take?

Let It Heal

Listen to the song and let it tell you how
be quiet be quiet be still
let the angels put their hands on where it hurts and
smooth be quiet be still
ask for prayers around you and bathe in song
be quiet be quiet be still
sit in children's laughter twice a day
be quiet be quiet be still
leave your thoughts for another time
wrap yourself in daylight
knit yourself a friend tighter than you imagined
let good people close to you
move away from those that suck from you
be safe be quiet be still

if you have no hands
write
if you have no feet
walk
if you have no voice
sing
and a chorus will carry you
if you have no eyes
see
if you have no arms
hug
be thankful be quiet be still

and the pouring come upon you like holy water
and the healing a new plant

break the ground
emerge clean and willing
sorry and thankful
new and quiet
rejoice
like children at kickball
wise like grandmothers on the stoop
ready to live
and whole
ready
and whole

Healer

You are a healer
like me don't be ashamed
no matter what is in your fingers you will bring it to people
french thyme and apple mint cherry roots blackberry leaves star
        apple words
your lips whatever
Listen to me child get it right what I'm saying
You have whispers the good ones that flow into the heart and stay
        like lace
light enough for someone not to feel you
graceful enough to add peace
intricate enough to add beauty

You are a healer of the highest kind
one who loves her patients
Don't matter what is in your hands how small or soft or wrinkled
You bring peppermint to the scalp and warm hands to the
        stomach
fawn's ear to the cheeks and breeze
You massage the necks and kiss throats open again
a beautiful occupation and dangerous

Don't take in bitter sweat
Breeze your hands over scars that refuse to go away
keep away from biting sores they will make you bleed
Don't challenge yourself into the fire that will swallow you whole
you are not that strong/maybe one day
For now you build your spirit with the small things

You will be doing this all your life from this world to the next
        to the next

you have time to perfect all your talents
Don't rush your fingers into broken bones don't rush your palms
         into slices

You can walk on fire
but ask for the soles of your ancestors
you can drink volcanoes
but ask for the throats of your mothers who spit fire as well as
         swallow it
you can walk below water
but ask for the lungs of your grandfather Ibo who know the way

All I ask child is never see you alone
We are always with you
If you see you alone you will die
and we will lose one of our necessary children
who we have not taught
so long for this fight
just to be extinguished

The Journey

is a song
black feet protruding the dust covering the water
falling into our souls
the journey is a prayer
find all of us in your song of this world
bringing it closer to where you want it to be
No mind the blood no mind the sweat
babies come and carry on
we do from back when
we do from far forward

The journey did not start from the castles or Middle Passage
it came from us black in the pupil of God's eye
large as the sky and sweet in the humming of the planets
let us carry on
we all pray
the old ones who have been here
the young ones who are not born
we wish to carry your song forward
in all the colors of the earth
if not us who would know blue
who would know the kindness of the sun
who would know green and healing
who would know ice in the waters and fire in the sands
we are the people planted first because we last the longest child
our heart with more depths than Atlantis
we hold the kingdoms lost

pray God we continue singing
pray God we continue the ways of the sticks and the undergrowth
          beneath our feet

pray God we know the waters
pray God pray God
pray God the journey finds us strong as we ever were as we always
   were
pray God the children know which way to go
pray God they recognize each other
pray God the little feet have big ones to step in

The journey long the song to guide us
voices on the left on the right
Solomon's song and Isis's song together in chorus
thoughts and hums arms and angles
chests and necks unshackled
never clear from the path
pray God we see how beautiful we are
pray God we recognize each other
pray God we see ourselves in each other's eyes
pray God you are my harmony
and us walking this world together
teaching it peace teaching it peace
because we have known war

Aché Olumba Alegba Akan
Aché Oshume Lucinte Akan
Aché my little ones my coming my gone
Aché let it be Lord let it be
we recognize each other in our journey
hold each other when we fall
keep company when we run
sing when we stumble
blow when we dust

drink when we rain
pray we bring water to this earth
it is so dry Lord it is so dry
and the little elbows paint the land in your smile
and the little feet dance your song unafraid
and the eyes see each other
and the ears hear your words
and the mouths speak love alone
in a crowded country of your children called this world
we the blood of your breath
the skin of your hope
stones of your fury
tears of your pain
hold your heart in our blues
your joy in our dance

Let the journey continue
let us speak the same language in our many tongues
may the path lead us home may the journey lead us home
in faith child let it be
in faith mother let it be
in faith pop pop
in faith sister
brother my brother let it be let it be
we the sky we the laughter of the rivers
we know day we know dawn we know evening
pray we know ourselves
pray I find myself in you
pray I find me in God
then I know where I'm going and feet to get there

The journey long y'all the journey long
but we got company
pray we find it
know it like our hands
we share
leave it to no one else leave it to no one else
because we took it before time was born
and end it when time is after

Aché little one
Aché

Classified #7

who will gather
the shards of my heart
hold them with two warm palms

my hands don't reach
these arms too long

i stand
in pieces
the world winds
around
sometimes slow sometimes fast
sometimes slow
sometimes
i walk praying
the rattle of this heart not so loud
for people to hear

sit
in a block of sun listening
for warmth on my skin
worst times can't get out of bed
for fear this heart cracks even more

tried tape and glue
even Divine thread from God's lovers
but i fear
i need two hands
to make a home inside my center
keep pieces of this heart together
like two palms in prayer.

We Walk

a bridge
between our parents' dreams
and vultures
between death's fingers
and the palms of the universe

Kin

Buffalo burned sage
steel jaws around the ankle
high prayers lowered foreheads high noon
these days gone
with my ancestors now long passed

who to carry them
when everyone claim his head too full
who to carry the story
of true things

we walk
empty armloads too full for treasure
thus the old winds must find a new way
into our children's ears

Risk

You cannot discover
new oceans
unless you have courage
to lose sight of the shore

Ilya Kaminsky

In these prayers and elegies deep anguish can be felt. When Ilya Kaminsky reads his poems you can hear this anguish coming through. Chris Abani says,

> When Ilya Kaminsky reads, the poem is wounded.
> An animal crying in the face of an approaching angel
> whose voice blends with its own—

Some say this is an influence of the old Russian poets with their incantatory reading style. Others say it is because he has been deaf since age four. Or is it a combination of both? Either way, Abani nails it. We are reminded of the opening to Rilke's first Duino Elegy.

> Who, if I cried out, would hear me among the angels'
> hierarchies? and even if one of them pressed me
> suddenly against his heart: I would be consumed
> in that overwhelming existence.

Author's Prayer

If I speak for the dead, I must leave
this animal of my body,

I must write the same poem over and over,
for an empty page is the white flag of their surrender.

If I speak for them, I must walk on the edge
of myself, I must live as a blind man

who runs through rooms without
touching the furniture.

Yes, I live. I can cross the streets asking "What year is it?"
I can dance in my sleep and laugh

in front of the mirror.
Even sleep is a prayer, Lord,

I will praise your madness, and
in a language not mine, speak

of music that wakes us, music
in which we move. For whatever I say

is a kind of petition, and the darkest
days must I praise.

Dancing in Odessa

We lived north of the future, days opened
letters with a child's signature, a raspberry, a page of sky.

My grandmother threw tomatoes
from her balcony, she pulled imagination like a blanket
over my head. I painted
my mother's face. She understood
loneliness, hid the dead in the earth like partisans.

The night undressed us (I counted
its pulse) my mother danced, she filled the past
with peaches, casseroles. At this, my doctor laughed, his grand-
daughter
touched my eyelid—I kissed

the back of her knee. The city trembled,
a ghost-ship setting sail.
And my classmate invented twenty names for Jew.
He was an angel, he had no name,
we wrestled, yes. My grandfathers fought

the German tanks on tractors, I kept a suitcase full
of Brodsky's poems. The city trembled,
a ghost-ship setting sail.
At night, I woke to whisper: yes, we lived.
We lived, yes, don't say it was a dream.

At the local factory, my father
took a handful of snow, put it in my mouth.
The sun began a routine narration,
whitening their bodies: mother, father dancing, moving

as the darkness spoke behind them.
It was April. The sun washed the balconies, April.

I retell the story the light etches
into my hand: *Little book, go to the city without me.*

Stranger

...Inhabitant of earth for forty-something years
I once found myself in a silent country

where human beings move, but how differently they move!
I do not know what silence is, mine or

not mine, this country speaks to me.
I am seated before an enormous typewriter. Outside—

a street café, the customers drink lemon vodka,
throw their cups in the air,

they speak of gratitude, the music
we touch in ourselves. If they have nothing else, silence

is their music. And here I stand, a fool in an old-fashioned hat,
I have earned the laborious right

to love my country: yes, I stop and stare
as the wonder of the sun occurs—

pigeons rise over churches, the opera theater.
How bright the sky is, as the avenue spins on its axis,

how bright the sky is (forgive me Lord) how bright.

Envoi

"You will die on a boat from Yalta to Odessa"
—A fortune-teller, 1992

What ties me to this earth? In Massachusetts,
the birds force themselves into my lines—
the sea repeats itself, repeats, repeats.

I bless the boat from Yalta to Odessa
and bless each passenger, his bones, his genitals,
bless the sky inside his body,
the sky my medicine, the sky my country.

I bless the continent of gulls, the argument of their order.
The wind, my master
insists on the joy of poplars, swallows,—

bless one woman's brows, her lips
and their salt, bless the roundness
of her shoulder. Her face, a lantern
by which I live my life.

You can find us, Lord, she is a woman dancing with her eyes closed
and I am a man arguing with this woman
among nightstands and tables and chairs.

Lord, give us what you have already given.

Of Deafness

Each man has a quiet that revolves
around him as he beats his head against the earth. But I am
        laughing

hard and furious. I pour a glass of pepper vodka
and toast to the white wall. I say we were

never silent. We read each other's lips and said
one word four times. And laughed four times

in loving repetition. We read each other's lips to uncover
the poverty of laughter. And whoever listens to me: being

there, and not being, lost and found
and lost again: Thank you for the feather on my tongue,

thank you for our argument that ends,
thank you for my deafness, Lord, such fire

from a match you never lit.

A Toast

If you will it, it is no dream.
—Theodore Herzl

October: grapes hung like the fists of a girl
gassed in her prayer. *Memory,*
I whisper, *stay awake.*

In my veins
long syllables tighten their ropes, rains come
right out of the eighteenth century
Yiddish or a darker language in which imagination
is the only word.

Imagination! a young girl dancing polka,
unafraid, betrayed by the Lord's death
(or his hiding under the bed when the Messiah
was postponed).

In my country, evenings bring the rain water, turning
poplars bronze in a light that sparkles on these pages
where I, my fathers,
unable to describe your dreams, drink
my silence from a cup.

Paul Celan

He writes towards your mouth
with his fingers.

In the lamplight he sees mud, wind bitten trees,
he sees grass still surviving this hour, page

stern as a burnt field:
Light was. Salvation

he whispers. The words leave the taste of soil
on his lips.

Elegy for Joseph Brodsky

In plain speech, for the sweetness
between the lines is no longer important,
what you call immigration I call suicide.
I am sending, behind the punctuation,
unfurling nights of New York, avenues
slipping into Cyrillic—
winter coils words, throws snow on a wind.
You, in the middle of an unwritten sentence, stop,
exile to a place further than silence.

*

I left your Russia for good, poems sewn into my pillow
rushing towards my own training
to live with your lines
on a verge of a story set against itself.
To live with your lines, those where sails rise, waves
beat against the city's granite in each vowel,—
pages open by themselves, a quiet voice
speaks of suffering, of water.

*

We come back to where we have committed a crime,
we don't come back to where we loved, you said;
your poems are wolves nourishing us with their milk.
I tried to imitate you for two years. It feels like burning
and singing about burning. I stand
as if someone spat at me.

You would be ashamed of these wooden lines
how I don't imagine your death
but it is here, setting my hands on fire.

Marina Tsvetaeva

In each line's strange syllable: she awakes
as a gull, torn
between heaven and earth.

I accept her, stand with her, face to face.
—in this dream: she wears her dress
like a sail, runs behind me, stopping

when I stop. She laughs
as a child speaking to herself:
"soul = pain + everything else."

I bend clumsily at the knees
and I quarrel no more,
all I want is a human window

in a house whose roof is my life.

A Toast

To your voice, a mysterious virtue,
to the 53 bones of one foot, the four dimensions of breathing,

to pine, redwood, sworn-fern, peppermint,
to hyacinth and bluebell lily,

to the train conductor's donkey on a rope,
to smells of lemons, a boy pissing splendidly against the trees.

Bless each thing on earth until it sickens,
until each ungovernable heart admits: I confused myself

and yet I loved—and what I loved
I forgot, what I forgot brought glory to my travels,

to you I traveled as close as I dared, Lord.

That Map of Bone and Opened Valves

That was the summer we damned only the earth.
That was the summer strange helicopters circled.
We spoke with our hands in the air
It is the air. Something in the air wants us too much.
On the second day
the helicopters circle and our legs run
in the fever-milk of their own separate silences.
A sound we do not hear lifts the birds off the water where a woman
takes iron and fire in her mouth
Her husband is trying to make
sense of her face, that map of bone and opened valves.
The earth is still.
The tower guards eat sandwiches.
On the third day
the soldiers examine ears of bartenders, of accountants,
      of soldiers.
You wouldn't know the wicked things silence does to soldiers.
They tear Pasha's wife from her bed like a door off a bus.
On the sixth day, we damn only the earth.
And my soul runs on two naked feet to hear Vasenka.
I no longer have words to complain my God
and I see nothing in the sky and stare up and
clearly I do not know why I am alive.
We enter the city that used to be ours
past the theaters and gardens past wooden staircases and wrought
      iron gates
Be courageous, we say, but no one is courageous
as a sound we do not hear lifts the birds off the water.

For B.T.

61

My Mother's Tango

I see her windows open in the rain, laundry in the windows—
she rides a wild pony for my birthday,
a white pony on the seventh floor.

"And where will we keep it?" "On the balcony!"
the pony neighing on the balcony for nine weeks.
At the center of my life: my mother dances,

yes here, as in childhood, my mother
asks to describe the stages of my happiness—
she speaks of soups, she is of their telling:

between the regiments of saucers and towels,
she moves so fast—she is motionless,
opening and closing doors.

But what was happiness? A pony on the balcony!
My mother's past, a cloak she wore on her shoulder.
I draw an axis through the afternoon

to see her, sixty, courting a foreign language—
young, not young—my mother
gallops a pony on the seventh floor.

She becomes a stranger and acts herself, opens
what is shut, shuts what is open.

Malena Mörling

How can we help but acknowledge the visible and invisible things that surround us, the things with which we've created and junked up our world?

> Two days ago 300 televisions
> washed up on a beach in Shiomachi, Japan,
> after having fallen off a ship in a storm.
> They looked like so many
> oversized horseshoe crabs
> with their screens turned down to the sand.

When Whitman says, "All truths wait in all things," we tend to focus on *truths* and *things*. But it is that they *wait* that seems important to me. When we recognize that "every word has a story / and every stone," then there is no disconnect, and the truths found there are immediately accessible. Mörling says, "I was not separate from anything living, I was / equally there and there was nothing to wait for."

A Story

The swallows have a story
they tell no one,
not even the rats,
the rats you once saw standing
on their hind legs
at the dump
late in the dark,
the car silent.
Not even the empty shopping cart
of the wind
as it wheels through the foliage—
Everyone has a story,
like a string of invisible Christmas lights
wound into the heart.
And every story has a story
that hides inside its own labyrinth.
The past has a story
as wide and as deep as the world.
Every word has a story
and every stone.

Happiness

How far away is your happiness?
   How many inches?
How many yards?
   How many bus rides to work
and back?
   How many doorways
and stairwells?
   How many hours
awake in the dark
   belly of the night
which contains
   all the world's bedrooms,
all dollhouse-sized?
   How far away is your happiness?
How many words?
   How many thoughts?
How much pavement?
   How much thread
in the enormous sewing machine
   of the present moment?

An Entrance

If you want to give thanks
but this time not to the labyrinth
of cause and effect—
Give thanks to the plain sweetness of a day
when it's as if everywhere you turn
there is an entrance—
When it's as if even the air is a door—

And your child is a door
afloat on invisible hinges.
"The world is a house," he says,
over lunch as if to give you a clue—
And before the words dissolve
above his plate of eggs and rice
you suddenly see how we are in it—
How everywhere the air
is holding hands with the air—
How everyone is connected
to everyone else by breathing.

For Max

Never Mind

"I am going to walk right out into Autumn—"
        the guy next to me
on the airplane said as we were landing.

Never mind that he had no legs.
        Never mind
that walking was no longer part of him.

Walking itself had walked off—
        with its heavy
combat boots and all the shoes

he had ever worn down to the first pair.
        Continuing its descent,
the plane banked downward and tilted

to the East and again he looked down
        at the earth—
at the shifting roof of the brilliant

yellow and orange foliage. He looked down
        at the meandering silver
of the river and at the road
        as if it were waiting for him.

In the Yellow Head of a Tulip

In the yellow head of a tulip
in the sound of the wind entangled in the forest
in the haphazard combination of things
for sale on the sidewalk
an iron next to a nail-clipper next to a can of soup
next to a starling's feather
in the silence inside of stone
in tea in music in desire in butter in torture
in space that flings itself out in the universe
in every direction at once without end
despite walls despite grates and ceilings
and bulletproof glass
the sun falls through without refracting
in the wind hanging out its own sheets
on all the empty clotheslines
in the bowels of rats
in their tiny moving architectures
in a world that is always moving
in those who are unable to speak but know how to listen
in your mother who is afraid of her own thoughts
in her fear in her death
in her own derelict loneliness
in the garden late at night
between the alder tree and the ash
she rocks herself to sleep in the hammock
a little drunk and wayward
in everything she is that you are not
in the well of the skull
in the fish that you touch
in the copper water
in its breath of water

in your breath, the single bubble rising
that could be you
that could be me
that could be nothing

Maps

It is freezing in the periodical room,
it's the hall of a train station
where people in their overcoats sit waiting.
The sun flames the dust particles
above the tables and slowly warms
the brown and dark green surfaces.
You are sitting between an elderly man with a
large book
of maps in front of him and a girl of fourteen
with a terrifying cough who writes her lessons
in the hand of a spider.
There is also a nun
in a brown dress and a loosely knit cardigan,
moving her lips as she reads,
perhaps memorizing the shape
of each sound, the way the blind
hold a word for every sight within.

A Father to His Son

"You know," a father said to his son:
"you didn't come with instructions—
I am taking care of you the best way I know."
The son, who was just nine
looked stunned below the blue rim
of his baseball cap.
He directed his eyes
with both a sense of surprise
and floating wonder
at his father.
They were sitting at the counter
of The Venus Diner on West 53rd Street,
having finished their evening meal.
Outside, people and cars drifted past
like unacknowledged thoughts
as the first dark of evening
ironed out every last crease of light
in every nook and cranny of the city.

My Shadow Falls Out of My Body

When the sunlight curves
   around the bend
of the mountain
     and the first shadows
fall out of the trees
   and hit the ground,
I remember waking early
     when I was seven
in our old house
   I'd look at the shadows
of the things in the rooms
     to see how they'd fallen
from the tall glasses
   still with some gin in them
on the kitchen table.

Visiting

In the shape of a human body
I am visiting the earth;
the trees visit
in the shapes of trees.
Standing between the onions
and the dandelions
near the ailanthus and the bus stop,
I don't live more thoroughly
inside the mucilage of my own skull
than outside of it
and not more behind my eyes
than in what I can see with them.
I inhale whatever air
the grates breathe in the street.
My arms and legs still work,
I can run if I have to
or sit motionless purposefully
until I am here and I am not here
the way death is present
in things that are alive
like salsa music
and the shrill laughter of the bride
as she leaves the wedding
or the bald child playing jacks
outside the wigshop.

In a Motel Room at Dawn

Now the air is visible again, floating
through the room
like a liquid, like water
washing over the ruined furniture.
And washing also over my head
here on this pillow, here where many
other heads have rested
their orbits of thoughts
and slept or stayed awake listening
to the motorcycle riders rev their engines.
But now they are silent.
Now I hear only the wind suffering
in some shaft. When we die
will the thoughts stop coming,
stop telling us what to do
next? Before you took
your own life, did you think
"now I will never see the sky"
or "now I have done all the dishes
I will ever do?"
Did you say "now my shoes will forget
how heavy I was" or "now….?"
Now everything is where it was left.
On the front desk the ledger lies open
showing the names of the guests
in the elaborate handwriting
of the clerk, and what it costs to sleep.
And now the maps of the earth
are resting folded
in the darkness of glove compartments,
all the arbitrary borders touching.

Standing on the Earth Among the Cows

When I was driving through Wyoming
past fields of just-overturned earth
black in the noon sun
and past thousands of cows
totally at home in the open,
I stopped the car to stop moving
and got out to stand among them
and I said nothing in English or Swedish.
Now I want to be whoever I was at that moment
when I discovered my own breathing
among the cows' breathing in the field
and studied their satin bellies
and udders slowly filling with milk.
I was not separate from anything living, I was
equally there and there was nothing to wait for.

For Elena

If There Is Another World

If there is another world,
I think you can take a cab there—
or ride your old bicycle
down Junction Blvd.
past the Paris Suites Hotel
with the Eiffel Tower on the roof
and past the blooming Magnolia and on—
to the corner of 168th street.
And if you're inclined to,
you can turn left there
and yield to the blind
as the sign urges us—
especially since it is a state law.
Especially since there is a kind of moth
here on the earth
that feeds only on the tears of horses.
Sooner or later we will all cry
from inside our hearts.
Sooner or later even the concrete
will crumble and cry in silence
along with all the lost road signs.
Two days ago 300 televisions
washed up on a beach in Shiomachi, Japan,
after having fallen off a ship in a storm.
They looked like so many
oversized horseshoe crabs
with their screens turned down to the sand.
And if you're inclined to, you can continue
in the weightless seesaw of the light
through a few more intersections
where people inside their cars

pass you by in space
and where you pass by them,
each car another thought—only heavier.

Kevin Goodan

Kevin Goodan grew up in Montana on the Flathead Indian Reservation, which is roughly 2,000 square miles of forested mountains and valleys just west of the Continental Divide. He worked for the U.S. Forest Service for a time and lived on a small farm in Western Massachusetts. In his poetry there is a real connection to the land, "near the heart of happening." Mary Oliver says that his is "a voice that connects joy with holiness, and sorrow with mystery, and all of this in a language as sharp as flint and as earthborn as the lamb." His language is sharp indeed, and his attention is equally acute, to the point of terror: "Terrifying / is the clarity by which I see…" We know he is sincere when he says, "The Lord is a place / to dig down into." Kevin Goodan probably has more dirt under his nails than any other poet writing today.

Theories of Implication

It begins in the leaves,
a hush that precedes all weather.

A cool light that sharpens the scene.
The air, the barn

empty of birds.
The tractor not moved for days.

Aspen along the low field, by the creek,
say nothing all night

and they say nothing now
which is the truth I'm after.

The culvert has its own theory.
So does the salt house

and the half-tub of molasses
caked with mud.

With the grass trying to maintain
the hue of September

everything is almost as it should be.
A new scent has entered the pasture—

an urgency that tempts like oats beneath a trough
for now I am come home

but all gates are left undone—
all windows empty.

Near the Heart of Happening

The foal hangs halfway out
and the mare strains
but can't push anymore.
I bring a bucket of cold river water
across the field. Haboo
I say in her ear,
what the Skagit children said
when the storyteller stopped:
keep the story going.
They said it with clamor,
with hands and voices
louder each time
but I am soft with it,
cool water on her neck.
Haboo I say reaching in
where the hips have locked
as she groans and falters.
Haboo for the shanks I grab
and jerk, for the spine
popping and the hips coming free.
Haboo for the foal lying in the dirt
as the mare nudges
and cleans its body
as the breathing stops.
Haboo as the body cools
as we stay with it after
as light begins,
as I regard the still air,
the meadowlark, the weight
of its bright singing.

Between Brightness and Weight

Frost on the white barn
but not on the red.
Frost on alder more white
than on thistle and dung.
Against snow in the pasture
where I walk clicking
my tongue among many sparrows rising.
Between brightness and weight.
How in trees wind turns air silver.
Ice on the water trough,
ewes breathing against it.
Green oak smoldering on a burn pile—
smoke more white than frost—
the whiteness of farewell—
the difference between snow untrampled
and sparrows over churned-up snow—
shadows deep and rough-hewn.
A mare coming slowly forward—
leaning into me when I scratch her neck.
The smell on my hands after.

If I'm Not a Garden

I'm in the pasture calming down the mares,
calculating what might be taken
by the hurricane as sacrifice.
Anything not rooted might be taken.
If I'm taken? There is a power in me
I do not understand. Terrifying
is the clarity by which I see,
as though each thing ignited by candles
inside. If I'm not a garden,
but a shadow pleading for stone,
rock, tree, or standing wall to cast against
in order not to vanish,
what then? The air is crisp. Sheep click their teeth
on blades of grass. Does vanish mean
to arrive elsewhere? A place perhaps
to flourish, to withstand? Maybe Freiburg
among the almost perfect German forests.
Maybe Ohio.

Gearing Housed in Twilight

You know it's a question of fortune
that I concern myself with birds.
Not as structures of ornament
or discord
as the trumpets in Mahler,
but as the actual augury.
The soft whirring in the nests
that bring forth morning,
cardinals, doves,
kestrels and kites,
and the cruelty
that I am equal to.
The ham-hammering
of those variegated wings
into the thing
behind the thing.
As I am with geldings,
with moonlight.
As the miner's life depends
upon the constant
singing of the canary
to bring him down and up again.
Like Audubon.
Or Cameron, dying, his mind
filling with the trumpets
of his rare swan. Because
nothing lasts.
Not even lasting.

Losing Something Important

You hear ice tightening in trees—
great birds driving through the wilderness.
And when the beasts shift in their stables
it is with a steadiness that once belonged
to paradise. Plant me in your soil she said
and I will become your earth.

Saudade

And what is given in return?
There was a darkness then
shaped by swallows—
a brightness given completely
by a few thistles and the moon.
But who's to say if the heart lives up
to what's placed in it?
Soon the trees will alter—
the earth grows small and bare.
Surely everything tender
is not granted. There is silence
among crickets meaning storm—
I spread flame in the windrow
to vetch the underbrush
but not damage the spruce
as I glimpse your face from
across the fire. The roaring heard,
the burning.

Snow Angels

The barn is a story we've taken refuge in,
the one where the ghosts never arrive.

We wait anyway
since the weather demands it.

Strike a match and nothing disappears,
nothing leaps out, either.

Snow is a verb with certain ideas in mind,
it settles on the fringe of your coat.

Give me your hands.
The wind has a way of saying things

no longer self-evident.
Since the barn does not repeat itself

I will. Your hands,
they are remote and necessary.

With the temperature this close to zero
everything is at risk.

This is not a story
we can leave untouched.

How the Soil Dampens for the Loss of Thee

My horses do not wander the pasture.
The skreep of a bird, far and hidden
In gray inflections across the landscape.
One eye of every beast is closed lightly.
Silver lines of slugs on the road-grit.
Some dark shape in the mist
Some dread thing emerging, and soon
The rain. My horses are not
My horses. The barn a borrowed thing
From a time I do not remember,
The sudden hallucinations of the lost
Where any direction becomes home.
Some kind of holding pattern
That allows me no peace. My horses
Were never horses. Which is
The world I have left. The delicate
Cheek-bones of the misbegotten.

We Pass and They Pass and Slow the World Abides

In harvest I was lost.
Listened for threshers,
Combines veering,
Hoping to grow near them,
Or the blade that keels loam
For winter. I stood still long enough
To see history and each bird,
The ones that appear
Tattered from some journey
Which is their final going,
Those that will reach
The end. Of what is given,
A restless shifting through the day.
Who you are I know not
But who are you to doubt
That what is true is temporary,
An audible click in the brain,
Or a stress of air through the throat
No easy inheritance.
Do you want to outride
The riders of your life?
I was lost and it had rained,
Harvest mashed and mouldered,
And it was going to rain
In the midst of acts of salvage
As the lush earth we knew once
And journeyed through
Settles back into clay.

August

The Lord is a place
to dig down into.
To harvest and burn,
let go fallow—
row of potato plants
blooming, thick
shocks of sweet corn
in rain, zucchini,
alfalfa,
carrots and fresh dung,
tobacco
steaming in a night.
In the five years
since you went away
I have not looked
for the Lord.
Tonight where I walk
He comes to me.
Fifty acres of wheat
past golden,
cardinals on a wood gate
silent, hands
waiting to open
like thistles in a pasture
more silver than air,
or coyotes in a windbreak,
a pen of sheared sheep.

In Chesaw Falling Behind

Orchard: nets of starlings rise.
Rain shakes loose—

ghost-seeds
in a ghost month.

A man from the far end sings
a language I do not know—

pours diesel in old tires,
sets to pruning branches.

And I, I lie on my back,
hands in gravel. I close my eyes.

Smoke wafts apple wood, then cherry—
and what the song says

I say. Wet weeds
soak into me one sprig at a time.

A fence screeks, tightens
and a herd bawls by.

He steps on a ladder—I know it's wood
by the way it doesn't ring out.

Branches drop to the fire.
A few stray bricks pop in the crackle.

In fields behind

schick, schick, schick of sprinkler pipe—

I sit up—listen for echo.
What the wind does, slowly, I do.

Jay Leeming

At the onset of the 21st century we have grown accustomed to morbid sensation, noise pollution, violence, cheap entertainment, and outdated republican values. Many poets, following the Language and postmodern poets, have come under the spell of fragmentation and obliqueness as a response to all this, which too often results in poetry for poetry's sake. William Stafford says, "People want even their entertainments to satisfy their lust for fear, cynicism, and disgust." We are no longer entertained. We've blurred the line between entertainment and fulfillment. Poetry for poetry's sake does nothing to heal. It plays dangerously close to the destructive thrills mentioned above. Like an ingrown toenail, it will eventually become infected. What we long for is a return to human feelings, a sense of awe. We are pleasantly surprised by the calm voices that speak deeper truths without ranting or lapsing into sentimentalism, like the moment when the boat touches shore at the end of "Rowboat." Just beneath the humor and surrealism is a cutting seriousness that pierces the heart. Robert Bly says, "[Jay Leeming] is a high-stepper, and he risks a lot with each brief line… His wit does not prevent him from writing things that move the reader."

Rowboat

An oar is a paddle with a home. This arrangement seems awkward at first, as if it were wrong; the wood knocks in the oarlock, and would much rather be a church steeple, or the propeller of an old airplane in France. Yet as it bites deep into the wave it settles down, deciding that the axe and the carpenter were right. And you, too, are supposed to be sitting this way, back turned to what you want, watching your history unravel across the waves as your legs brush against the gunnels. Your feet are restless, wanting to be more involved. But your back is what gets you there, closer to what finally surprises you from behind: waves lapping at the shore, the soft nuzzle of sand.

Apple

Sometimes when eating an apple
I bite too far
and open the little room
the lovers have prepared,
and the seeds fall
onto the kitchen floor
and I see
that they are tear-shaped.

Two Months After

A clutch of rain against the windows.
All day this beaten house has been bearing up
under the March wind, a wind that aches
down the thick beams the carpenter cut

to take its weight. A mud-covered truck
drones up the hill, under a stone sky.
Spring will come only after the hard work
of the water is done, after the high

green leaves have shouldered their sparks
through the winter's ancient test.
Perhaps then the hard ice of your death

will have rotted away. In Schubert's songs
I listen for your listening, for the arc
of smoking notes your night-heart sang.

Organic Music

Red columns through which smoke
strays and marches, stone on stone
gathering with age a talk
full of cats' eyes, a house of bone
where we pray to the sky in which a ship
burns. Book of moon and fire,
book of the black seeds kept
within laughter, inside the voice of the choir
standing on the earth made of tears.
I place a coin on the ladder
of pain's wealth, lay my hands
on mother, father; the surf
rinses us clear to new dirt, a sound
holding the year in dark sand.

I Want to Go Back

I want to go back beyond the chicken bones
and the piled garbage bags of Brooklyn in August,
back beyond the ring on her finger
and the party years ago
where I met her fierce, unpleasant husband
for the first time;
back beyond even the warm confusion
of her long body and blonde hair
on the bare mattress of a Saturday;
back to the moment when we lay down sweating
in the cricket-heavy darkness
with our heads together
and the music of the dance we'd left
burning just out of reach behind the trees,
to when we did nothing but breathe
as the northern lights
loosened their vapors across the stars.

Law Office

I am sitting in an adjustable chair on the 32nd floor of a skyscraper in New York City. I am typing a list of a thousand names into a computer. As I work I am listening through headphones to a recording of the journals of Cabeza de Vaca, a Spanish explorer who traveled to the United States in the 15th century. The office is air-conditioned and I am wearing a tie. A hurricane has drowned half of de Vaca's crew, and most of the rest are sick and dying of starvation on an island off the Florida Keys. The names I am entering are plaintiffs in a case against Union Carbide chemical company, and about half of them are deceased. Some filing cabinets are behind me; one is marked "Bhopal" and another reads "Breast Implants." The secretary sitting beside me goes to get a cup of coffee. De Vaca and his crew have eaten their horses, and are now sailing in a makeshift raft that uses their hides for sails. I keep typing. At noon a man comes through the office and waters all the plants. Every hour another sailor dies of pneumonia, or loses his grip and slides off the raft into the storm.

Supermarket Historians

All historians should be supermarket cashiers.
Imagine what we'd learn;
"Your total comes to $10.66,
and that's the year the Normans invaded Britain."
Or, "That'll be $18.61, the year
the Civil War began."

Now all my receipts are beaches
where six-year-olds find bullets in the sand.
My tomatoes add up to Hiroshima,
and if I'd bought one more carton of milk
the cashier would be discussing the Battle of the Bulge
and not the Peloponnesian War.

But I'm tired of buying soup cans
full of burning villages,
tired of hearing the shouts of Marines
storming beaches in the bread aisle.
I want to live in a house
carved into a seed
inside a watermelon—
to look up at the red sky
as shopping carts roll through the aisles
like distant thunder.

The Light Above Cities

Sitting in darkness,
I see how the light of the city
fills the clouds, rosewater light
poured into the sky
like the single body we are. It is the sum
of a million lives; a man drinking beer
beneath a light bulb, a dancer spinning
in a fluorescent room, a girl reading a book
beneath a lamp.

Yet there are others—astronomers,
thieves, lovers—whose work is only done
in darkness. Sometimes
I don't want to show these poems
to anyone, sometimes
I want to remain hidden, deep in the coals
with the one who pulls the stars
through a telescope's glass, the one who listens
for the click of the lock, the one
who kisses softly a woman's eyes.

She Killed the Spider

She killed the spider
that I've been watching all summer,
the one whose grey bedsheets flapped
in the corner beside the mailbox.
I liked coming home
to that web spun by the door,
to the spider hiding in the corner
and the gnats caught in the web
like mail.

Now it's autumn, and the nights are cold.
I value every name
in my address book
even more.

For Robert Bly

I Pick Up a Hitchhiker

After a few miles, he tells me
that my car has no engine.
I pull over, and we both get out
and look under the hood.
He's right.
We don't say anything more about it
all the way to California.

Grandpa Putting Salt on His Ice Cream

He would hold the salt shaker
in his right hand, and tap the end
over the dark chocolate.
"It enhances the flavor," he would say.
He had more ice cream in his life
than his ancestors ever did, and more butter,
and more milk, and more eggs.
And when these things filled his veins
and pulled him down,
when the barn of his heart caught fire,
it was those ancestors that his eyes
rolled back to see;
strong Norwegian brothers
driving their cows out of the fields
towards the market and the city,
towards railroads and electric lights,
towards world wars and cameras,
towards his body, his thoughts
and his life.

Song of the Poison in the Executioner's Needle

I am all the determination of the State wrenched
into a vial, a nail for the heart, a chemical axe
for the body
and its great tree of blood.
I cannot hear radios or violins,
families, guns
or money. Do not tell me
about mother's milk, about your laws
bent towards harmony
or revenge. I could not have bandaged the cuts
the handcuffs dug in his wrists
as he struggled. I could not have said
his name. I could not have sat down beside him
and explained why it was necessary
for him to die.

Terrance Hayes

"Poetry is the language of suggestions not the language of meaning."
Terrance Hayes knows that meaning will be different for each reader
and not kept in the poet's head for readers to puzzle out. Elsewhere
he says, "Tone may be a better word than meaning. Tone in
"Mystic Bounce" feels tangled and tangential, abstract and blue—
but not without pleasure. Where the other poems involve the real-
ities of dream, it involves the jagged dream of reality. I think my
work vacillates between these two poles. One foot permanently
buried in the mud, the other permanently levitating an inch or two
above ground." His is one of the most powerful and uniquely orig-
inal voices of our time. This is why Terrance Hayes is included
here. Most poets either snuggle up to the corpse of Sylvia Plath or
Robert Lowell or attempt to levitate with Khalil Gibran. The good
ones understand Jiménez:

> My feet, so deep in the earth!
> My wings, so far into the heavens!
> —And so much pain
> in the heart torn between!

Wind in a Box

This ink. This name. This blood. This blunder.
This blood. This loss. This lonesome wind. This canyon.
This / twin / swiftly / paddling / shadow blooming
an inch above the carpet—. This cry. This mud.
This shudder. This is where I stood: by the bed,
by the door, by the window, in the night / in the night.
How deep, how often / must a woman be touched?
How deep, how often have I been touched?
On the bone, on the shoulder, on the brow, on the knuckle:
Touch like a last name, touch like a wet match.
Touch like an empty shoe and an empty shoe, sweet
and incomprehensible. This ink. This name. This blood
and wonder. This box. This body in a box. This blood
in the body. This wind in the blood.

Talk

like a nigger now, my white friend, M, said
after my M.L.K. and Ronald Reagan impersonations,
the two of us alone and shirtless in the locker room,

and if you're thinking my knuckles knocked
a few times against his jaw or my fingers knotted
at his throat, you're wrong because I pretended

I didn't hear him, and when he didn't ask it again,
we slipped into our middle school uniforms
since it was November, the beginning

of basketball season, and jogged out
onto the court to play together
in the vision all Americans wish for

their children, and the point is we slipped
into our uniform harmony, and spit out *Go Team!*,
our hands stacked on and beneath the hands

of our teammates and that was as close
as I have come to passing for one
of the members of The Dream, my white friend

thinking I was so far from that word
that he could say it to me, which I guess
he could since I didn't let him taste the salt

and iron in the blood, I didn't teach him
what it's like to squint through a black eye,
and if I had I wonder if he would have grown

up to be the kind of white man who believes
all blacks are thugs or if he would have learned
to bite his tongue or let his belly be filled

by shame, but more importantly, would I be
the kind of black man who believes silence
is worth more than talk or that it can be

a kind of grace, though I'm not sure
that's the kind of black man I've become,
and in any case, M, wherever you are,

I'd just like to say I heard it, but let it go
because I was afraid to lose our friendship
or afraid we'd lose the game—which we did anyway.

The Blue Etheridge

Dear Parole Board of the Perennial Now,
let me begin by saying it's very likely
none of my ex-wives will vouch for me.
Let's just say the parable
of the Negro who uses his dick for a cane
and the parable of the Negro who uses his cane
for a dick convey the same message to me.
I'm sorry. You mean before that?
Well, it's as if some ghost the height
of my granddaddy was lighting a cigarette
the wrong way to symbolize my muddy path
through life. You ever seen the Mississippi?
You'll learn all you need to know
if you look at the wall of my kinfolk's pictures.
Belzora. BuShie. My sisters. Me
and my brothers fishing in high waters.
Whenever I see brown hills and red gullies,
I remember what the world was like
before I twisted spoons over flames.
I pissed from a bridge the day I left.
Yes Sir, I've changed, I've changed.
But I won't be telling you the story
of the forlorn Negro or the Negro cutthroat
or the Negro Hero or the Negro Tom.
I won't be telling you the story of the night
I died. I believe everything comes back
to music or money. Belly Song.
Song of the twelve-fingered fix.
Song of The Gemini Women. I know I'm cursed.
I sang out to the Baptists I saw gathered
on the riverbank the day I left. I sang out

to the reeds straight as tongues and the salmon
in the waters of my people, and beyond that
to my barrel-backed shadow damming the stream.

The Blue Terrance

I come from a long line hollowed out on a dry night,
the first son in a line of someone else's children,
afraid of water, closets, other people's weapons,
hunger and stupidity, afraid of the elderly and the new dead,
bodies tanned by lightening, afraid of dogs without ethos,
each white fang on the long walk home. I believe all the stories
of who I was: a hardback book, a tent behind the house
of a grandmother who was not my grandmother, the smell of beer,
which is a smell like sweat. They say I climbed to the roof
with a box of lightbulbs beneath my arm. Before the bricks,
there were trees, before the trees, there were lovers
barely rooted to the field, but let's not talk about them,
it makes me blue. I come from boys throwing rocks
bigger than their fists at the head of the burned girl,
her white legs webbed as lace on a doily. In someone's garage
there was a flashlight on two dogs pinched in heat.
And later, a few of the puppies born dead and too small
to be missed. I come from howls sent up all night and all day,
summers below the hoop and board nailed to a pine tree.
I come from lightbulbs glowing with no light and no expressions,
thrown as far as the will allows like a night chore, like a god
changing his mind; from the light broken on the black road
leading to my mother. Tell me what you remember of her
now that her walk is old, now that the bone in her hip strains
to heal its fracture? I come from the hot season
gathering its things and leaving. I come from the dirt road
leading to the paved one. I will not return to the earth
as if I had never been born. I will not wait to become a bird
dark enough to bury itself in midair. I wake up sometimes
in the middle of the country with fur on my neck.
Where did they bury my dog after she hung herself,
and into the roots of what tree are those bones entangled?

I come blessed like a river of black rock, like a long secret,
and the kind of kindness like a door that is closed
but not locked. Yesterday I was nothing but a road
heading in four directions. When I threatened to run away
my mother said she would take me wherever I wanted to go.

Wind in a Box

—After Lorca

I want to always sleep beneath a bright red blanket
of leaves. I want to never wear a coat of ice.
I want to learn to walk without blinking.

I want to outlive the turtle and the turtle's father,
the stone. I want a mouth full of permissions

and a pink glistening bud. If the wildflower and ant hill
can return after sleeping each season, I want to walk
out of this house wearing nothing but wind.

I want to greet you, I want to wait for the bus with you
weighing less than a chill. I want to fight off the bolts

of gray lighting the alcoves and winding paths
of your hair. I want to fight off the damp nudgings
of snow. I want to fight off the wind.

I want to be the wind and I want to fight off the wind
with its sagging banner of isolation, its swinging

screen doors, its gilded boxes, and neatly folded pamphlets
of noise. I want to fight off the dull straight lines
of two by fours and endings, your disapprovals,

your doubts and regulations, your carbon copies.
If the locust can abandon its suit,

I want a brand new name. I want the pepper's fury
and the salt's tenderness. I want the virtue
of the evening rain, but not its gossip.

I want the moon's intuition, but not its questions.
I want the malice of nothing on earth. I want to enter

every room in a strange electrified city
and find you there. I want your lips around the bell of flesh

at the bottom of my ear. I want to be the mirror,
but not the nightstand. I do not want to be the light switch.
I do not want to be the yellow photograph

or book of poems. When I leave this body, Woman,
I want to be pure flame. I want to be your song.

Wind in a Box

Even the dirt dreams of it now.
It is two roads along two rivers,
The sky above a mother's face

The day her husband leaves
For war. No blood and stars
But the blood and stars.

Let's find it and break its fucking neck,
Let's break its fucking jaw.
Let's break its fucking ganged in vessels

And if it pushes back and a tiny blue rises
On its cheek, let's break that too
Until stars dance in the corners

Of its eyes like white seeds
And let's break those too
Until all the words we know are split in two.

No power but the power of need.
Let's get up ready to feel.

God bless the rage in us.
It's how we know each other.
We who keep vigil by the windows,

We who pour ashes from the windows
Into the wind, skin passing over skin.
Let's walk up the hill and along the rows

That do not ask questions.
Near the white and yellow flowers,
Strangers are moored in sighs.

Soon it will rise without kissing
Anyone goodbye.
It says we will not be renewed,

We will not be filled
Like the birdhouse.
It says we will arrive unwashed.

Aren't you tired? Let's lie down.
Let's cry out and rest.

Wind in a Box

I claim in the last hour of this known hysterical breathing,
that I have nothing to give but a signature of wind,
my type-written handwriting reconfiguring the past.

To the boy with no news of my bound and bountiful kin,
I offer twelve loaves of bread. Governed by hunger,
he wanted only not to want. What is the future

beyond a premonition? What is the past
beyond desire? To my brother, I leave a new suit, a tie
made of silk and shoes with unscuffed bottoms.

To the mirror, water; to the water, a book with no pages,
the author's young face printed on the spine.
I wanted children taller than any man on earth.

If everyone was like me, I said to the mirror.
To my lover, I leave enough stories to fill an evening.
Enough sleep to walk from one coast to another

without pause. I held no counsel with God.
I cut open the fruit of a tree without speaking to the tree.
I ate food prepared by strangers. To the black cashier,

I leave nothing. Her story is like the one I was given.
To all the carpenters looking at the ceiling, nothing.
Here in the last moments of my illiterate future,

may the people know I did not matter.
Shoeprints at the door. Shoeprints on the old road.
To the boy with two lights going on and off in his stare,

I leave the riddle of the turtle who had shelter,
but no company. To the black girl, grace. To the black girl,
mirrors; a father blessed with the gift of mind-reading,

men who do not wound her, men she does not wound
herself for, and mother love. Unable to shed the old skin
and stand, I stand here in the hour of my hours alive.

These words want to answer your questions.
These words want to stave off your suffering,
but cannot. I leave them to you. Enough sky

and a trail. Wood and enough metal for machines.
Tell me, what am I going to do when I'm dead?
Let my shadow linger against the earth, protect my children.

Threshold

No steps remained, but we did not leap
from the knee-high grass of that house
abandoned in the woods to the porch

with the planks that were as loose and warped
as those of a small boat beached long ago
by someone who rowed one last time

from a lake in a kind of reverse drowning,
the kind that calls one permanently to land
when someone has been lost, the water opening

indifferently and closing in the same manner
until even the oar strokes were traceless,
the boat left to become more and more

vaguely like the ribs of something that lived once,
that had purpose, but now could not hold a body,
could cradle nothing except the occasional rain

and wind the way the body cradles breath—
the warped, narrow wood of the porch
reached beyond us, me and the daughter of a man

who had been like me, who had been young
when this house was new and warmed by people
we would not ever know except by way of a black sock

someone had used to wipe away shit or semen
and left in the corner before going out again
to the porch and yard to sink

into the will of whatever else makes up the woods.
Seeing the sock then told me some of the possible history
of the world around us: that others had come here,

probably the girl's older brother had been hiding here
while their father knocked at almost every door
in our neighborhood looking for him one night,

and maybe the cool somber-jawed dropouts
had been here, and other couples
who could not afford hotels,

others had left crushed and uncrushed cans
and clouded bottles, stick porn and mottoes
and aliases on the walls; they'd left their smell there too

and the roof seemed to want to guard it
though when the windows were smashed,
the doors kicked open, some of their musk

had been swept into the woods where it met the two of us
approaching with nothing but our caution
and green irrevocable hunger, and we could see it

would not hold us, the old porch,
so we did not leap from the knee high grass
to get in, we stepped as lightly as others had crossing

planks that splintered and cried out
as if to the old house and maybe to the deep, deep woods
and to the path others had not intended to leave.

Cocktails with Orpheus

After dark, the bar full of women part of me loves—the part
      that stood
naked outside the window of Miss Geneva, recent divorcée who owned
a gun, O Miss Geneva where are you now—Orpheus says she did

not perish, she was not turned to ash in the brutal light, she found
a good job, she made good money, she had her own insurance and
a house, she was a decent wife. I know descent lives in the word

decent. The bar noise makes a kind of silence. When Orpheus hands
me his sunglasses, I see how fire changes everything. In the mind
I am behind a woman whose skirt is hiked above her hips, as bound

as touch permits, saying don't forget me when I become the liquid
out of which names are born, salt-milk, milk-sweet and animal-made.

I want to be a human above the body, uprooted and right, a fold
of pleas released, but I am a black wound, what's left of the deed.

Clarinet

I am sometimes the clarinet
your parents bought
your first year in band,
my whole body alive
in your fingers, my one ear
warmed by the music
you breathe into it.
I hear your shy laugh
among the girls at practice.
I am not your small wrist
rising & falling as you turn
the sheet music,
but I want to be.
Or pinky bone, clavicle.
When you walk home
from school, birds call
to you in a language
only clarinets decipher.
The leaves whistle
and gawk as you pass.
Locked in my skinny box,
I want to be at least
one of the branches
leaning above you.

Mystic Bounce

Even if you love the racket of ascension,
you must know how the power leaves you.
And at this pitch who has time for meditation?
the sea walled in by buildings. I do miss
the quiet, don't you? When I said, "Fuck the deer
antlered and hithered in fur," it was because
I had seen the faces of presidents balled into a fist.
If I were in charge, I would know how to fix
the world: free health care or free physicals,
at least, and an abiding love for the abstract.
When I said, "All of history is saved for us,"
it was because I scorned the emancipated sky.
Does the anthem choke you up? When I asked
God if anyone born to slaves would die
a slave, He said: "Sure as a rock descending
a hillside." That's why I'm not a Christian.

Stick Elegy

The dead were still singing *Turn the lights down low*
Beneath Yellow Bridge where years before, clowning
And ass out, Stick jumped with nothing but the State
Championship trophy in his righteous clutch. The water
Was supposed to be deepest there, and for three seasons
Straight MVPs: Charlie "Fly" Kennison, Long Timmy Long,
And Rocket Jefferson, those are the names I knew, jumped

Free. But Stick's ankle broke. I fished him out, crumpled
And bawling like the day he was born, like an object of
Baptism, and a life of bad luck followed in the shape of
Floods and fractured lightning, and then, numb, tooth-
Less, and changed, the dead refused burial, striking out, 2
By 2, 4 by 4, from the morgue house to raise trouble at
The bridge. I started hearing birds everywhere after that.

Luljeta Lleshanaku

If there is an owner's manual on how to live in this world causing as little destruction as possible, it has been written and continually revised through stories and poems. Yet we don't seem to learn much from them.

Perhaps I am too pessimistic. I think this way often, but these thoughts dissipate when hundreds of Blanchard's cricket frogs leap before me as I walk the edge of a pond, or I smell the first lilacs of summer. Luljeta Lleshanaku reminds us that, "There is no destiny, only laws of biology," then observes, "fish splash in water / pine trees breathe on mountains."

Lleshanaku was born in Albania in 1968 during a crucial turning point in that country's history. Her poetry is clear and original partially because she is of the generation of poets following the collapse of the harsh Stalinist dictatorship in 1990 that had virtually no contact with the literature of the outside world.

One of her translators, Henry Israeli, says, "The lines of her verse that fell so softly, naturally onto the page carried an immense sadness." He goes on to say, "What she hungers for is true contact, compassion, conversation." It is this longing, this immense sadness, we sense in her poems.

Memory

There is no prophecy, only memory.
What happens tomorrow
has happened a thousand years ago
the same way, to the same end—
and does my ancient memory
say that your false memory
is the history of the featherhearted bird
transformed into a crow atop a marble mountain?
The same woman will be there
on the path to reincarnation
her cage of black hair
her generous and bitter heart
like an amphora full of serpents.

There is no prophecy, things happen
as they have before—
death finds you in the same bed
lonely and without sorrow, shadowless
as trees wet with night.

There is no destiny, only laws of biology;
fish splash water
pine trees breathe on mountains.

Waiting for a Poem

I'm waiting for a poem,
something rough, not elaborate or out of control,
something undisturbed by curses, like a white raven
released from darkness.

Words that come naturally, without aiming at anything,
a bullet without a target,
warning shots to the sky
in newly occupied lands.

A poem that will well up in my chest;

and until it arrives,
I will listen to my children fighting in the next room,
and cast my gaze down at the table,
at an empty glass of milk
with a trace of white along its rim,
my throat wrapped in silver
a napkin in a napkin-ring,
waiting for late guests to arrive....

And the Sun is Extinguished

And the sun is extinguished
like the little red light that disappears
when the elevator stops.

I can't remember which is our floor—
the third, fifth, or the hundred and first...
but it always ends the same way:
a slap of cold air
the look of impatience
on the faces of those
waiting to get on.

Child of Nature

No one noticed me
at my parents' wedding—
my face scrunched
as if I had eaten sour fruit—
tucked away like a wet invitation in a pocket.

Soon thereafter,
my mother swung the window of her chest shut
and opened a larger one on her belly,
overlooking the street
in the morning
as the scent of fresh coffee
and toast wafted in.

She knew what she desired
I was her pure, perfect objective,
I, who humbly flew from her body,
a magpie with a diamond in its throat,
a novel read aloud, beginning on the last page.

The newly opened jars of cream
in her dresser drawers
were out of bounds for me,
as were the unblemished perfumes and powders,
lipstick the size of a finger
pointing seductively to exotic places.

I was there until the very moment
chromosomes were combined—
a handful of hazelnuts with a handful of ginger—
but not a moment later.

More than a Retrospective

I was born of a dead hope
like a sprig of grass
between sidewalk slabs.

I learned my first words
behind an ill-fitted door.

I came to understand
the properties of light and darkness
through the cracks in my body
a clay body not wholly fired.

I learned to sing
the way a cold draft learns to navigate
between two clumsy lovers.

But like a whore's dirty underpants
I am not growing used to sadness…

One dead hope
catches up to the next
like one bus approaching another
then the stop.

Sunday Bells

My soul
beats like a tongue
against the side of a bell.

Listen.
It's the Sunday bells
the Sunday bells of high mass
when the priest preaches forgiveness
and we all lay flowers on graves.

Monday in Seven Days

I.

Monday feels like an odd shoe,
its other chewed by the dog tied at the gate.
The sun always rises through the open backdoor
and pours into the house like birdfeed along the street.
Men returning from the pebble beach,
walking with their hands held behind them
on their way to nowhere
look like crosshairs on a gun,
their spit still bitter with coffee,
dandruff scattered along their collars;
to draw them you would have to hold your breath.
For weeks now there hasn't been a single drop of rain. The thin
                              stream dwindles, sickly, syphilitic.
A child skipping school
sneaks away from his mother.
He is nine and still adds and subtracts on fingers
                              blackened by fresh walnuts,
counting the years to his conscription.
He draws a large dusty circle in the dirt
that looks like a piece of blighted flesh
where a tumour had just been removed.

II.

Like salmon, ready to mate,
swimming upstream from the sea
to the river's estuary
the wedding guests step backward in time

and beg the landlady to return their flesh:
"Mine is bright white…"
"Mine is soft, with a burn from a hot iron on my forearm…"
"Mine smells of sage, like a canvas bag…"
"Mine is magical, you can wear it inside out…"
"Give me anything—it doesn't matter!"

Here comes Mustafa, the drunkard,
with his head stuck to his body's right side.
He is Monday's Saint, guilty of everything,
absorbing everyone's sins
like a swab of alcohol dabbed cotton
pressed to a wound.

III.

Before sleep the world returns whole beneath eyelids,
an army full of pride gathered under the Arc de Triomphe,
the loot of war behind them.
The nightly rite of fucking,
that shredded music
sufficient to hide
the motive for which we woke up this morning
and, even more so, the motive to wake up tomorrow.

The lamp turns off for the last time
and blood continues on its small circular route.

IV.

When my grandma came here as a bride
with nothing more than her good name,
the house was empty but for the hanging weapons.
There was so little here she had to build a whole town
just to find a pair of shoulders for a head.
She began by planting an apricot tree in front of the house
and later another, so that the two were
as hands cupped to a face
to warm it.
Then children dripped from her,
rain from a tin awning.
Those who fell on soft ground were forgotten.
Those on cement
managed to survive.
To this day
they still stand petrified in a black and white photograph,
in woollen suits with oily unevenly cut hair
looking uncomfortable,
looking as if their lives were borrowed from elsewhere.

V.

Broken toys were my playthings:
zebras, wind-up Chinese dolls, ice-cream carts
given to me as New Year presents by my father.
But not one was worth having.
They looked like cakes whose icing had been
                    licked off by a naughty child,

until I broke them, cracked and probed their insides, the tiny
                                    gears, the batteries,
not aware then that I was rehearsing
                        my understanding of freedom.

When I first looked at a real painting
I took a few steps backwards instinctively
                                    on my heels
finding the precise place
where I could explore its depth.

It was different with people:
I built them up,
loved them, but stopped short of loving them fully.
None were as tall as the blue ceiling.
Like in an unfinished house, there seemed to be a plastic sheet
                    above them
                                instead of a roof,
at the beginning of the rainy autumn of my understanding.

VI.

Here is the honest man, the just man,
his face a picnic blanket
shaken of crumbs.
His kind never remains unemployed.
He asks, "Does anyone have a nail to drive into
the hole in my chest?"

My great-grandfather was like that,
and so was my grandfather and my father.
Maybe if I were a son I would have been the same,
staring up at a *worthless* father
(What a shame! I'd say).

"How far should I go?" the son would ask only once.
"Until you lose sight of yourself."
It might have been a dream,
because his family tree was struck down by

                                     a bolt of lightning
and then the pleasing scent of *uluweah*

                                     spread over the village.

VII.

The smell of roots in the air, and the rain falling
like bees returning to their hive, all at once.
It's a tradition in my family to distinguish happy rain from
          melancholy rain
conceived above hilltops during summer.
I listen with one ear, waiting as if for the moment one recognizes
          that a stranger's voice
is indeed one's own voice.

My uncle asks for a *"fazzoletto"* to wipe his glasses.
He has used that word since the time he went to Florence
to have his pneumonia cured—a time he remembers
as fondly as a honeymoon.

With my report card in his hand,
veins throb at his temples—a matter of life or death.
He is the one to determine
whether I will be a brick for a wall
or a stone for a barn.
The hand that he hits with
is an instruction manual read only once
although the furrows on his palm—the limits of his destiny—
are the only things which
don't leave scars on me.

"To hell with it! Bring me *un fazzoletto!*"

VIII.

If you had dark skin
your smile would be exquisite,
neither incomplete nor flashing rotten teeth.
F. knows this. She mourns for her son.
Early in the morning she opens the window,
lights the kerosene stove
with a piece of crumpled telegram still in her hand,
sweeps the yard, feeds the chickens,
cooks for ten,
fixes the chair with the sphinx's arms
opposite the door.
And each day
with the claws of a hawk she fights against
disorder,
begging for form and discipline

like the square plots of a field of wheat
guiding the part of herself which flies mercilessly
in a straight line,
never landing.

She accepts greetings with her eyes
and pathways open before her
like the Sabbath among other days,
dedicated to gratitude and prayer.

IX.

As is said in Latin, *Medio tutissmus ibis*[1]
The embroidered tablecloth in the middle of the table
The table in the middle of the carpet.
The carpet in the middle of the room.
The room in the middle of the house.
The house in the middle of the block.
The block in the middle of the town.
The town in the middle of the map.
The map in the middle of the blackboard.
The blackboard in the middle of nowhere.

Lola is an angel. Her forehead hasn't grown since she was eight,
her centre of gravity unchanged. And she likes edges, corners,
although she always finds herself
in the middle of the bus
where people rush towards the doors at either end.

My neighbours never went to school,
nor have they heard of aesthetics,
and hardly have they ever read anything
about the Earth's axes, symmetry, or absolute truth.
But instinctively they let themselves drift towards the middle
like a man laying his head upon a woman's lap,
a woman who, with a pair of scissors,
will make him more vulnerable than ever
before the day is done.

X.

Preparing for winter
isn't tradition, but instinct. We hurl our spare anxieties
like precious cargo from a shipwreck.

Taedium vitae[2] is a time zone
that no longer exists.
The smell of boiled beans separates us
from our neighbours, a dream above the stove
separates us from our ancestors.

There isn't a middle-man
between me and my talents.
The wind preaches with the nasal voice of a false prophet.

Years somersault over frozen slopes,
and we instinctively hide our heads between our knees.

Limits wither away. My body,
more abstract than ever, is a country without an anthem,
a country, delirious and once near death, which I touch
like a mother touching her lips to the forehead of her child
with a high fever.

1 The middle is the safest ground
2 Supersaturation with life, satiety

The Mystery of Prayers

In my family
prayers were said secretly,
softly, murmured through sore noses
beneath blankets,
a sigh before and a sigh after,
thin and sterile as a bandage.

Outside the house
there was only a ladder to climb,
a wooden one, leaning against a wall all year long,
ready to use to repair the tiles, in August before the rains.
No angels climbed up them,
and no angels climbed down them,
only men suffering from sciatica.

They prayed to catch a glimpse of Him,
hoping to renegotiate their contracts,
or to postpone their deadlines.

"Lord, give me strength," they said,
for they were descendants of Esau,
and had to make do with the only blessing
left over from Jacob,
the blessing of the sword.

In my house praying was considered a weakness,
like making love.
And like making love
it was followed by a long night
of fear
so alone with the body.

The Bed

My bed, a temple
where murmurs of a stifled prayer press
against my palate.

Frozen genitalia
buried fruit, imperfect fruit
clean green leaves stretching out beneath the blankets

to reach you, your warmth
dew on the skin of a morning dream.
A mole like a coffee bean on your back
arms that rarely hold me
and my eyes, rocks of salt
brought ashore by the tide.

My bed is not a bed, but a temple:
we change sheets as often
as the religious replace candles.
We leave our shoes in a neat row outside the door.
The heads of sacrificed birds roll up the stairs
to where we are throbbing, a single being split in half
martyred by silence.

Out of Boredom

Out of boredom
roebucks lie down with toads
night swallows the moon
like a sleeping pill
and sky becomes lace
on the veil of a dreamer.
A white strand of smoke rises
like a cypress
from a burning cigarette.

The clock tower warbles a soldier's old tune
the one he whistles as he polishes his steel crutches.
An old woman's fingers, anxious as a child's
held out for a nickel, tap a tarot card.

Out of boredom
footsteps consume the streets
with the hunger of Chaplin in a silent film.
Out of boredom the soul, like an amoeba,
expands and divides
so that it will no longer be alone.

Nocturne. Soft Whistle

Now I imagine you, mother,
as you nap, snoring, one breast
sunk like a moon into sweet waters.
Are you frightened by thoughts of the insulin
the doctor prescribed this morning?
My little, old mother
past tense
or future past
wrapped inside the gray shawl
of an acrylic poem.

Sleep is short
there is hardly time
to dream about what life once held for you:
one white child, one black child
chasing a ball of yarn along the rug.

I know the way you startle awake.
I know the shattered door
at the entrance to your glass house.

But don't let me disturb your nap
with the swirling of my imagination,
a flock of zinc birds flying low to the ground.
Even in my dreams I cannot quell
the waves slapping against the hull
of a boat that follows the current.

Sherwin Bitsui

Like Trickster in these poems, Sherwin Bitsui catches us off guard and forces us to view the world from an angle we aren't entirely comfortable with. As I mentioned earlier, the danger for us is when we attempt to keep Trickster energy at bay. Remember, Trickster—in this case raven or coyote—moves between heaven and earth, and between the living and the dead, and always shows up when we least expect him to. As Jon Davis says, his poems "move by deep intuition. Bitsui haunts the edges between cultures, connecting the previously unconnected, finally dissolving the boundaries between worlds."

Atlas

Tonight I draw a raven's wing inside a circle
        measured a half second
            before it expands into a hand.
        I wrap its worn grip over our feet
            as we thrash against pine needles inside the earthen pot.

He sings an elegy for handcuffs,
        whispers its moment of silence
at the crunch of rush-hour traffic
and speaks the dialect of a fork lift,
        lifting like cedar smoke over the mesas
            acred to the furthest block.

Two headlights flare from blue dusk
        —the eyes of ravens peer at
Coyote biting his tail in the forklift,
        shaped like another reservation—
            another cancelled check.

One finger pointed at him,
that one—dishwasher,
he dies like this
        with emergency lights blinking through the creases of his
        ribbon shirt.

A light buzzed loud and snapped above the kitchen sink.
I didn't notice the sting of the warning:
        Coyote scattering headlights instead of stars;
howling dogs silenced by the thought of the moon;
constellations rattling from the atmosphere of the quivering gourd.

How many Indians have stepped onto train tracks,
    hearing the hoofbeats of horses
    in the bend above the river
       rushing at them like a cluster of veins
    scrawled into words on the unmade bed?

In the cave on the backside of a lie
soldiers eye the birth of a new atlas,

one more mile, they say,
                one more mile.

Blankets of Bark

Point north, north where they walk
in long blankets of curled bark,
dividing a line in the sand,
smelling like cracked shell,
desert wind, river where they left you
calling wolves from the hills,
   a list of names
growling from within the whirlwind.

Woman from the north,
lost sister who clapped at rain clouds.
We were once there
holding lightning bolts
above the heads of sleeping snakes.

Woman, sister, the cave wants our skin back,
it wants to shake our legs free from salt
and untwist our hair into strands of yarn
pulled rootless from the pocket of a man
who barks when he is reminded of the setting sun.

At 5 A.M., crickets gather in the doorway,
each of them a handful of smoke,
crawling to the house of a weeping woman,
breaking rocks on the thigh of man stretching,
ordering us to drop coins into her shadow,
saying, "There, that is where *we* were born."

Born with leaves under our coats,
two years of solitude,
the sky never sailed from us,

we rowed toward it,
only to find a shell,
    a house,
        and a weeping woman.

River

When we river,
blood fills cracks in bullet shells,
oars become fingers scratching windows into dawn,
and faces are stirred from mounds of mica.

 I notice the back isn't as smooth anymore
        the river crests at the moment of blinking;
its blood vessels stiffen and spear the drenched coat of flies
collecting outside the jaw.

Night slows here,
        the first breath held back,
clenched like a tight fist in the arroyo under shattered glass.
But we still want to shake the oxygen loose from flypaper,
hack its veins,
divert its course,
        and reveal its broken back,

the illusion of a broken back.

Calyx

Kneeling before the altar of your hands
you close your eyes and listen to wooden sunbeams
splinter dirt floors into peninsulas of ice,
each crackle—
a fissure of crow wings fluttering past the stone
on which you sharpened your teeth,
as if cornering the wolves
snarling when you ask to leave your hair bandaged
would shut windows opened to green pastures
and plume your palm with brown skin.

*

Amber barn light flashes upon orange rinds worming through the
     cow's skull,

ivory columns of smoke followed by silk curtains billow from our
     flushed eyelids,

scattering snow over the cliff's edge, we know for some reason that
     the reason was here.

The night, our cornfield's glittering backdrop, splatters the wind-
     shield and we are flung

back towards dust, our minds forked with spilled ink tasting like
     turtle blood under our

hushed bodies.

✿

at zero hour
the poem spilling its seeds into your mouth
sunflowers a yield sign
and crawls onto the roof pinching corn meal.

✿

I compare my hands to
what I imagine *thought* might look like when suspended in fossilized
    amber and release the captured mosquito from my closed fist.

This windowless house marrows my veins with thinking
scraps of meat leaf the picture frame

How do I describe her daubing my face with cornhusk?

At Deer Springs

Turn signals blink through ice in the skin.
Snake dreams uncoil,
                      burrow into the spine of books.
Night spills from cracked eggs.
Thin hands vein oars in a canyon bed.
We follow deer tracks back to the insertion of her tongue.

Red Light

What was asked for
won't step into view.
Coyote jumps
        onto asphalt running west,
dreams reoccur,
lightning strikes
        the same nerve ending twice.

Bullet Wet Earth

Pushing back the whip
I tuck and roll,
darting again
   from the bullets that smell of wet earth,
monsoon earth
   rising like foam through the fences that wound.

Last night a thorn flowered the imagination of a thorn;
a moth buried its tongue between my fingernails,
and a calf was dragged the length of my body.

My shoulders hang like a rainstorm over a bed that has become
       desert
as I have become:
   a dehydrated shadow born with scratches in his throat.

It's easy to drift through this desert,
one hand on the wheel,
the other
   pinching dew drops into seeds that glide into vapor.

The doctor said it was a heart condition,
and it's been two years of listening to the wind and only wind
   that is making our bodies yearn to be suckled by black stones.

I cover these pages with my fist.
Imagine skin meeting the lens of a camera.
   Hear a voice coming from the roots in the basket, saying:

"Come closer,
swallow a handful of air,
    pour water over your feet,
    you have become a ghost without hands."

The Sun Rises and I Think of Your Bruised Larynx

Sister,
blue like the larynx of rushing rainwater,
I think of you when I squeeze static from the river's bent elbow.

I am counting:
ten to zero, zero to nothing
underneath the dawn oak
whose roots resemble your hair
after you've danced counterclockwise
around steel-rimmed America
and returned home
with back spasms and a foaming mouth.

Do you still want to bury your shoes
in the blues mountains west of the Rio Grande,
where white birds shout sunlight
        and people don't ask you to repeat your last name?

I tie my feet to the thinning hair of our old ones;
their eyes burn, staring into headlights of passing cars;
they saw footpaths bloom into black-boned factories,
rivers into pipelines,
and children delivered by IHS doctors
without tongues, without the fifth finger.

I think of your cupped hands tucked into the petals of a
        mud-caked sun.

The raven browned by the winter moon's breath
releases its wings,
        stretches its neck,

resembles for a second
the silhouette of a horse's head
carved from the nugget of coal
found in your grandmother's clenched fist.

from *Flood Song*

I walk my hair's length over tire ruts,
crush seedpods with thumbnails,
push kernels of corn
into dove nests on the gnarled branches of our drowned lungs.

Mining saguaro pulp from garden rock,
squeezing coarse black hair—
I arrive at a map of a face buried in spring snow.

With a plastic cup
I scrape the enamel chips of morning songs
        from the kitchen sink,
and breathe through my eyelids,
glimpsing the thawing of our flat world.

I dial into the blue skin of the map's stiff pulse,
emeralds spill from the skull's cavernous wail,
but nightfall is still darkest
in the middle stanza of the poem
        arcing twenty miles past forgiveness.

The poem
        held out to the wind
        speaks *juniper* to the wilderness,
as August slithers into September's copper pipes
searching for the paw-print of a waterfall
                        on the mind's lunar surface.

Here—I thread nightfall into the roan's black mane.

Here—I peel a paper mask from the hare's moist cartilage.
Here—tornadoes twist into the loom's black yarn,
but the premonition—
beginning with three masts and a cross—
still mushrooms over the groans of husbands and wives
folding their petals outward
from their salt-coated bodies
     saying . . . *nihi yazhi, nihaaneendza,*
       nihi yazhi, niha aneendza.

       our child, you have returned to us,
         our child you have returned to us.

Bodies Wanting Wood

When the fire turns
I lotion my arms
The woman weaves a storm design
Smells rain in the canyon floor

The wind in winter sleeps between our fingers
During prayer
It is released and blows into town
A swarm of locusts with wings on fire

The Four Directions of a Lie

1.

The rain
      mid-morning
scratching seeds from the marrows of bullets.

A brass door handle warms the palm of the intruder.

The suggested retail price of entrance
      hasn't yet cracked under the weight of our gravitational pull.

A pull to the nucleus of a lie.

Each nail extracted from the ships is driven into their palms
until they are only hands laid flat on the earth's buckled vertebrae.

2.

Two birds spit oil: sunbeam, soot, sunbeam . . .

3.

The rain clouds
      thoughts of milk—
books clam shut under the patter of blind children
    who cut their flesh with the hands of steel clocks
      and slide like melting ice underneath the church door.

But the door
with its fist full of light
wanted only daughters
        who would ripen during autumn,
            who would become the mothers of a drowned city.

4.

The last whisper heard this morning was not the shuffle of feet
nor the momentary pause in the tightening of his jaw.

It was the sudden leap of a deer when water rippled outward under
        his chin.

Some say it is *irony,*
others
        a bear twitching in the hunter's garden.

Trickster

He was there—
before the rising action rose to meet this acre cornered by thirst,
before birds swallowed bathwater and exploded in midsentence,
before the nameless
    began sipping the blood of ravens from the sun's knotted atlas.

He was there,
sleeping with one eye clamped tighter than the other,

        he looked, when he shouldn't have.

He said, "You are worth the wait,"
in the waiting room of the resurrection of another Reservation
and continued to dig for water, her hands, a road map,
in a bucket of white shells outside the North gate.

He threw a blanket over the denouement slithering onto shore
        and saw Indians,
leaning into the *beginning,*
slip out of turtle shells,
        and slide down bottle necks,
aiming for the first pocket of air in the final paragraph.

He saw anthropologists hook a land bridge with their curved spines,
and raised the hunters a full minute above its tollbooth,
        saying, "Fire ahead, fire."

When they pointed,
he leapt into the blue dark
        on that side of the fence;
it was that simple:

sap drying in the tear ducts of the cut worm,
his ignition switched on—

    blue horses grazing northward in the pre-dawn.

Maria Melendez

The energy in Maria Melendez's poems comes from both extremes: the spirit world of imagination and love and the underworld of dampness and the soul. "Spirit and flesh / will have sometimes had enough // of go-betweens."

In a time of spiritless materialism, Maria Melendez isn't simply writing a few interesting poems. She is casting the new images of mythology, and is creating a vessel that can contain them.

These aren't safe and tidy ideas. Melendez knows that the gray whale that swims under the sea of thought is not a charming whale of children's books but is scarred and barnacled. One feels the presence of grandiosity in her poems; there is no trace of dishonesty. Gary Snyder calls her an "eco-eros explorer." If the way to reach heaven is by first going through the earth, then Melendez is digging the right channel.

Remedio

Let go your keys, let go your gun,
let go your good pen, and your rings,
let your wolf mask go
and kiss goodbye
your goddess figurine.

There is a time to grip
your talismans,

a time to strip yourself of them.

Spirit and flesh
will have sometimes had enough

of go-betweens—

A refastening
of our noses and our ears

onto our soul

can only be accomplished
in the company of master exemplars.

Take wolves, each with a soul full of scents:

asperine willow leaves
and damp earth, willow-rooted.

At the end of summer, a wolf's soul hears

cottonwood catkins'
long trajectory down an ageless azimuth,

feels, in her inner ear,

myriad shifts of air
    as the tufty seeds ride twilit rays
        and glow as we imagine all
            eternal things to glow.

A remedy for when you've lost your sense
of Spirit in the world,

a simple spell for home lycanthropy:

    Smell the new season,
    acrid, tensed to grow
    in budding wolf willow,
    and feel the heat recede
    from a moose's corpse—then
    recuerda esta loba.

Recuerda. . .from the infinitive *recordar*
which is, at root, not remember or re-mind,

but pass back through the heart—

    let her pass back through your heart again,
    this wolf.

Note: Recent research points to the strong possibility that the reintroduction of wolves into Yellowstone National Park may be causing the increased vigor of streamside vegetation communities; these communities had previously been overbrowsed to the point of local near-extinction by elk and other ungulates. Wolf predation provides more scraps for scavenging coyotes, eagles, and other animals than do contemporary hunting practices by humans. See http://www.cof.orst.edu/wolves/ and http://nature.berkeley.edu/~cwilmers/.

Love Song for a War God

Every part of you contains a secret language.
Your hands and feet detail what you've done.
Your appetite is great, and like the sea
you constantly advance, lunge after lunge.

Unlike my brother sleeping in his chair,
you do not take reality with ease.
Your Pain builds up its body like a cloud
rotating its collage of hot debris.

O, Teacher! We have learned that all men's tears
are not created equal. We were wrong
to offer flames to quell your fires. Still,
I must dismember you inside this song.

Your mouth's dark cave awaits Victory's kiss;
blood is the lid your calm eyes never lift.

Tonacacihuatl: Lady of Our Flesh

—Sacramento Valley—

Fragrance of the rain in her breath. The dampness
at the back of her knees smells like rain also.
She appears with a shining crow the color of cinnabar,
and a mark at her shoulder blades displays the same crow.

Poison has made her throat lovely. For that poison,
praise is chanted in heat-meters making triple-digit noise.
Part of her has the form of a tule stem, and that form
she can absorb, if she wants it hidden. And it is hidden!

How many spirits she's twin to, and how long she'll last in this world,
are secrets stashed in the rattle
of corn ears, in the coils
of venomous snakes.

Thirteen mirrors spangle her dress. For those sun-round mirrors,
praises are chanted by thirteen thousand red-legged hoppers.
At noon, she steps out of a culvert and collides with the naked light,
and her fever is an affliction known as August.

So she is, Lady of Our Flesh, who is what is.
Is she not here, who is our mother?
Huffing, with matted hair, she stamps a shovel blade
to begin a small grave.

An Ocean of Code

I want to disappear like the glaciers.
> To hear the story I've misnamed "mine"
>> drip, like time, back into
>>> pebbly soil. Trying
to decipher who wrote these praises,
> spoke with crows, who made
>> this dent in mystery, solving
>>> for pattern, I break
a book spine with my foreign-
> sounding name on it...find nothing
>> but type and the same head-haze.
>>> The furthest out of the fog
I can lumber, today: spit-shining
> a smudge of food off my daughter,
>> my thumb rubbing wet circles
>>> on her cheek.
A bald eagle fledges from a bare
> cottonwood on the elk refuge,
>> eyeing the coyote crunching
>>> a yearling calf's carcass—
and on the plains, a wave
> of one-thousand cranes ululate con-
>> volute calls, gaze from the Eocene
>>> age to the dusky Platte muds.
A better poet would know
> what it means, all of it—clattering song,
>> the keel of it, the bloodied, scavenging
>>> teeth of it—I'm deaf on the floor
of an ocean of code, but still
> something globes, bubbles,
>> floats from my lips,
>>> rising to riddle the surface.

Between Water and Song

Many ancient *americano*
        calendars agree—

this era is on its way out.
        One prophecy

says the next world
        will be water,

another says
        mundo floral.

Do we have time
        to argue the difference

between flower and water,
        water and song?

Knot of Prayer

For the Buddha with his hand
                   down a little girl's pants

For the Christ who is fondling
                   her nipples

For the Heavenly Father settling
                   her fingers on his shaft

For the Ever, Everywhere
                   forcing into—

Be gone, be gone, be gone, be gone, gone beyond beyond.

The gasping furnace, the rasp
and clatter of face-wide leaves
scattering over the deck—we've
learned to move through
our new home's armory of sounds
without alarm, taming
jumpiness with mental labels:
a creaking here, a scratching there,
it's Normal, Natural.

We make a custom of raking,
get used to the heat-system's
raucous breath. I kill
and kill the same spider,
big hobo in the tub,

every morning—one
click forward in the mom-lock
of rituals turned each day
to block the children
from threat, the various venoms.

Next house over lives a code
violation, a criminal
record, an offender under
watch by State Corrections.

More than all the protective charms
and spells I wish I knew, I wish
I were a perfect guardian
beyond exhaustion every night—
three doors to check before sleep
and I'll forget one, guaranteed—
one of these nights, I'll forget.

———————————

What could be tied and waiting / at the stake?

My curled, my jumping

girl, six years of hair-
brushing, brother-
chasing, tiny one who sings into the face
of a stuffed tiger, she of cheeks
soft as sage leaves...

Home-page for the registry
lists his targets:
            Female, Child.

Home-page advises: be a good
neighbor, do not harass, offer
acceptance, support re-entry.

Such a sticky state!—asked to act as though
            it's human!

This tearing and breakage, this...

            him.

He likes to smoke on his porch step
across from my window.
He's out there every night
while I'm washing dishes.

A compassionate person would ask

what went wrong, to make him act this way?

I am not compassionate.

I am afraid—

to worship the Greatness
     when It stains the edge of soothing nights
     with sunlight meant to scald.

For the Roshi implacably asking me
     to let monsters live in peace,

For the Apostles reminding me
     to love my neighbor,

For the Hierarchs keeping quiet
     about monsters in their midst,

For the Cosmos' random collisions
     launching life,

     I clamp my teeth on this plea
     for selective banishment—for the halves of you
     who say it's damage that teaches,
     keep your half-hands the hell
     away from my girl.

     In the hot gold of autumn,
he mows the back lawn and talks to her—
we've only lived here two weeks.

     You can get used to anything. 14 pounds
per square inch pressure on your face, ("one atmosphere"),

the 12 pound melon at the end of the stalk of your neck.

I tell the kids "don't talk to him" and "run,"
now seeing him is more fun
than a sprinkler.

———————————

I have been so angry
at my children
that my teeth clatter,
a fist
within me
rattles my frame
as it fights to be
renamed.

———————————

I dreamed it was meth
   that did it, "thirteen years ago,"

and I dreamed his regret. He
   said, "That was

not me, not me." It was his face
   entering this plea,

as a prisoner who's hunched before a judge.
   His weathered cheeks, same

ash-blond hair, his mouth moving
but my voice.

One wants one's response to be firm,
immobile, frozen. As a mother, I have planned
to be consistent. Lord, let this fear
keep clenched in me, tight as February
buds grip their green secrets. Let me not
relax into blossom, Lord, unfold me not
unto your holy weathers.

Maybe other universes have flat
refugia, homages to stasis, planets
sure of their places. Not ours,
with its rotatious whirl and
orbit, we get tipped into July
every time.

Summer instructs us
in patience. Be still
and float over
afternoon fever—
night air will race through
to loosen ribbons
that braided heat tight
against the day.

A corpse, however wounded,
joins the root world, gets used to
the formative earth's
manifold pressures.

———————————

We're not used to that man, but he grows
spectacular vegetables.
My husband accepts
an armful of sweet onions—

"Come and pick plums anytime."

(Even the moon goes home and shuts her door
when her work in the garden's through.)

———————————

For the moon with her tongue
in the unwashed pans,
in the spider's jaws,
in the girl's ear—

Backcountry, Emigrant Gap

I thought we fell asleep
austere and isolated—

two frogs calling across Rock Lake.

By morning, deer prints
new-pressed
      in the black ground between our tents—

      more lives move beside us
      than we know.

Why Not Attempt the Summit

—Mount Shasta City, 1999

All night the buried mouths
    beneath our condos lecture us,
        we can hear their blather
    extrude up into the fir trees,
the diminishing clinks of words
    chiming minor keys
        on their way to the stars.
    Love as much as you
can, don't throw your heart
    away to just one god, wash
        the baby in mint, watch
    where you step on the mountain,
things that live so high
    don't want visitors.
        Feed them whiskey, concrete,
    cigarette or bone ash, doesn't matter,
nothing keeps them shut.
    So we trust their advice and vow,
        with our red and recycled breath,
    never to scramble or crawl above
the porous wall of trees
    that marks a crooked timberline
        along the gravel and scree.
    We'll only go far as the limber pines,
and won't presume to chase spirits
    over tinkling shales.
        We mind this limbed boundary
    because the town mechanic

crossed over it in a vision
        that almost killed him; andesite grains
                winked up at him from the highest slopes,
        and he drove into their dark fission
of mineral and glass;
        but when the valley drew his stone limbs down,
                the gravitational tow
        of his hoard of sleeping relatives
nearly tore apart
        his breath from bones, from heart;
                he tumbled out of the dream
        in a surge of scalding rock and scarlet vapors.
We don't tempt this verge
        because andesite is not a visionary's word,
                snow-wet andesite is
        metamorphic and too visionary,
and the tiny pink blooms
        of alpine Campanula (which deeply
                thinks to grow an inch
        each quarter century) would snare us
into slow, endless worship—
        our children would go hungry.
                (We know these perennials
        from stories that the dirt dreams up—)
We keep to our side of the trees
        because the firs themselves are near enough
                to provide sufficient comfort
        to subsist on, and so much
has already sloughed
        from the sure face of the land for us,
                and to learn the grace

in songs to praise the spiders
living that high, we'd have to die
or want to die and ever after hope
for nothing else but death.
Because the need to be self-referential
every instant above treeline
is lethally disorienting to us:
always having to look at one's
trunk to be assured of one's existence,
to look at oneself and not one's surroundings
to verify what one is.
In the alpine, only the winged
know who they are in reference
to shifting slopes; we're not shaped
to rise and flow on updrafts.
We live behind the scar
of this limit because there are no houses,
of devotion or otherwise, above
the timber; because we were created
in the firs' image and remain,
like the firs, unclassifiable;
we try to prefer
forest enclosure to Krumholz exposure
because we need to ask for nothing
from at least one space because great powers,
wild and hunted,
sought and supplicated to,
need a place to be left to themselves,
to their own devices.

Pleading erodes creators
       under any circumstance,
             and there are no perfect worshipers
       for these gods outside all measures of perfection.
They need a high, storm-cleansed
       refuge, sparkling with silence,
             to perch and preen on when valley air
       becomes polluted by exhausted ghosts.

An Argument for the Brilliance of All Things

On a downed spruce at Murie Ranch,
branches curve like scoured whale ribs,
moss adheres as seaweed would.

An old ruffed grouse struts through the windfall,
drumming, drumming
its courtship ritual.

Yet still we hear the claim "human consciousness
consummates," as though matter waits, barren,
for its better half.

Meanwhile, grouse sperm
have every confidence
in the messy interlock

of matter with matter.
If, indeed, consciousness could be
extracted from the mountains

like iron ore, isolated
from shale beds—as crude—siphoned out
from the center of cells

like messenger RNA, could be
examined on a slide plate,
ex situ,

we'd have to admit
that its saline content

matches that of the ocean, a tear,

a teaspoon of semen, a ferning
droplet of amnion waters.
Know this, all humanists:

under the pure, lifeless
surface of the Sea
of Thought swims a great

gray whale, scarred
and barnacled, carrying
a calf, a great gray whale

about to breach.

Ann's Answer

My best poet-friend finds an American quest for
                              inner peace

abhorrent.
She thinks all our nails, in wartime,
                    should be bitten down to bloody.
If the war seems far—
            all the more reason
                        to rend our garments.

        And I say:

Those who can stain their hands
                    with wild blackberries,
should.

Let those who remember the earnest part
                    of heat and orchards,

the companionable crack
                    of dry leaves under their feet,

let those called to answer cicada rustle
                    over the marshy water

alone.

For Ann Stanford, 1916-1987

Valzhyna Mort

Valzhyna Mort does not like to be called a Belarusian poet. Nor does she like to be called a political poet, a female poet, a young poet, or even a poet, for that matter. There is such fierceness and urgency in her voice that she worries every time she writes a poem it will be her last. Mort's poems are daring and electric. They are like a brief but powerful summer storm that leaves the streets steaming and the flowers trembling. There is a wry sense of humor reminiscent of Wislawa Szymborska in her work.

Mort's poems welcome duality. They embrace the idea of *both/and* as opposed to an *either/or* mindset.

> because we are children
> ali baba and *allahu akbar*
> are the same to us

My students pointed out that the color white appears often in her poems, connecting it to the spiritually pure, innocence, counter-revolutionary tendencies of her poems. But Mort is adamant that we notice her use of the color red as well. In "Snow White" the queen, dressed as a peasant, presents to Snow White an apple that is half red and half white, showing her the poisonous red side, eating the non-poisoned white side herself. When we select fruit from the produce isle, isn't it the most attractive pieces we choose first?

Teacher

if you are going to be my teacher
you will have to become a tiger
so that you can bite my head off
and i'd have to follow you everywhere
trying very hard to get my head back

For Linda Gregg

in the pose of a question mark

How hard it is to pull ourselves up
from the pose of a question mark
into the pose of an exclamation.
The left labia of Poland and the right labia of Russia part
and our heads emerge out of...
what?
By now we have sixteen names for snow—
it's time to come up with sixteen names for darkness.

In the pose of a question mark—
with our whole bodies we call ourselves into question,
confirmed by a dot of urine.
Is it us? Really? Calling into a question?
Or adolescence has just birthed
a rumpled beach towel.

So blunt were
the midwife's scissors
that with time they turned into
brightly-polished avenues
jointed by a military obelisk.
A tractor plant started manufacturing hair-rollers,
and every Sunday they sent mother
a gift basket.
Her head in rollers—
the ideal reconstruction of the solar system—
was photographed for albums and calendars.

The principle of rollers clenching hair
underlay the national production of harvesters.
This became my first metaphor

which I gobbled till my mouth foamed
as if I had swallowed the whole Swan Lake.

My body didn't belong to me.
Bent with pain,
it was making a career out of being a question mark
in the corporation of language.

The bureaucracy of the body drove me to the wall:
head didn't want to think—
      let the eyes watch
eyes didn't want to watch—
      let the ears listen
ears didn't want to listen—
      let the nose smell
nose didn't want to smell—
      let the hands touch
the body blooming with linden flowers of pain.

Where are my bees?
Aren't I sweet enough for them?

untitled

was it a hair you lost
one that's grown roots
when upon the sheet's desert
two bodies
fell like welcome rain

or were those snakes
startled awake in the caves of the blanket
snakes that stuck out
their fiery tongues
like a fountain of blood
the air died
strangled
between two bodies

white sea foam
this is what's become of the sheet
and the blanket waves tossed
two fishes on the floor
turning their mouths inside out
and what is that hanging there
if not a red half-moon
or was it god
who cast down his voice
and the voice struck my house like thunder
as frozen as lightning
from my bed
grows a single tulip

A Poem about White Apples

white apples, first apples of summer,
with skin as delicate as a baby's,
crispy like white winter snow.
your smell won't let me sleep,
this is how dead men
haunt their murderers' dreams.
white apples,
this is how every july the earth
gets heavier under your weight.

and here only garbage smells like garbage. . .
and here only tears taste like salt. . .

we were picking them
like shells in green ocean gardens,
having just turned away from mothers' breasts
we were learning
to get to the core of everything with our teeth.

so why are our teeth like cotton wool now. . .

white apples,
in black waters, the fishermen,
nursed by you, are drowning.

Juveniles

because we are children

between days and nights
as between adults' feet in a dance hall
painting our faces like easter eggs
slipping into one another's mouth
our tongues
like red envelopes
bribes

because we are children
ali baba and *allahu akbar*
are the same to us

unbelievers we are sincerely grateful
to christ for his blood
and each one is fully prepared
to pay a lot of money for it

because we are children
what could be worse?
the life we live—you'll never see anything like it, even in the movies

and summer our fat-ass nanny
is feeding us her sweet traffic jam
in the craters of cities whose names we're reciting

starting with *sir* in a whisper
because we are children
we are the sugar of the earth

and if we seem green
it's only on account of the traffic lights
but in an instant you will see
the lights will tear open their chests
revealing red hearts

because we are children
juveniles

and we fly all airplanes
and all airplanes fly to minsk
because we are children
no one is going to deny us the city we grew up in

Fall in Tampa

it's our blood that's dried up
and crumbles through our fingers
like faded leaves
but there is no fall in here
and summer is standing stock-still
like a white heron in green water

Belarusian I

even our mothers have no idea how we were born
how we parted their legs and crawled out into the world
the way you crawl from the ruins after a bombing
we couldn't tell which of us was a girl or a boy
we gorged on dirt thinking it was bread
and our future
a gymnast on a thin thread of the horizon
was performing there
at the highest pitch
bitch

we grew up in a country where
first your door is stroked with chalk
then at dark a chariot arrives
and no one sees you anymore
but riding in those cars were neither
armed men nor
a wanderer with a scythe
this is how love loved to visit us
and snatch us veiled

completely free only in public toilets
where for a little change nobody cared what we were doing
we fought the summer heat the winter snow
when we discovered we ourselves were the language
and our tongues were removed we started talking with our eyes
when our eyes were poked out we talked with our hands
when our hands were cut off we conversed with our toes
when we were shot in the legs we nodded our heads for yes
and shook our heads for no and when they ate our heads alive
we crawled back into the bellies of our sleeping mothers

as if into bomb shelters
to be born again

and there on the horizon the gymnast of our future
was leaping through the fiery hoop
of the sun

Opera

opera—
is a fish market
where fish sing with the silver of their flesh
the conductor plunges the knife
and from the nets of singers' lungs
deep-water fish fall out.
and when in agony on the cutting board
in a hysterical search for the sea water
it licks the sweat from its dealer's hands
and gulps the dripping on the floor blood
hoping to stuff it back in its body—
silver scales melt into a bullet
and the bullet aims at the fish's gills—
sing!
how could it know under the water
that it took from the hook not the bait
but a note
that a pole made by Stradivarius
would bite at its heart like a serpent
three times—
asana! asana! asana!
three chimes—
for farther, spirit and son.

who are you—a conductor or priest?

is it a baton or a cross?
sh-h-h-h!
opera!
not earrings your Carmen wears but tambourines
her heart like a horn lives off the lips

no blood in her veins but saliva of kisses
and blood she wears outside as a dress
oh Carmen! we smuggle out into night
the cargo you hid inside our ears.

don jose! slim like a knife's blade
you'll write the last note
on scores of the gypsy's ribs.

opera!
voice tasting on an empty stomach!
a vineyard
of your wardrobes!
I would run through it barefoot
into unknown lands
with a wasp in my ear!

violetta! a tree rose from your mouth
so where's its bird
to sing on the top
why did you tear out its feather
and stuff its body inside your chest
on the left

opera—you are injured darkness
on the audience body—the wound of the stage
and your sounds already flee the sinking ship.

but again and again the red curtain
parts like the red sea
in front of moses

and we walk ahead
into the last and longest note—
into silence.

EUGENE GLORIA

On the cover of Eugene Gloria's *Hoodlum Birds* is the lower half of El Greco's "The Burial of Count Orgaz." Painted in 1586, it hangs in the vestibule of the Church of Santo Tomé in Toledo, Spain. Catholic Spain at the time had its eyes turned upward toward the heavens rather than to the earth, and forward, to eternal life rather than an earthly one. Gloria conceals the upper half of the painting where Christ, the Virgin, angels and saints swirl in exulted movement and ecstasy with the soul of Count Orgaz, thus focusing on the stillness and grief of the earthbound mourners. This isn't meant as sacrilege to the great painter, rather a tongue-in-cheek artistic choice, while at the same time suggesting something in Gloria's poems. How often we concentrate on the afterlife and ignore the here-and-now, where a "husband mistakes happiness / for a loosened apron, a pear // ripening on the sill, / his wife's hair tucked behind an ear," where "the road, which suggests things, is tired of ceremony," where "grief straggles like a bottom-dweller." As Naomi Shihab Nye says, his is "a deep eye tuned to rich detail and melancholy." Upon first reading these poems are beautiful and rich, yet they suggest something more going on just beneath the surface. The joy of reading and rereading Gloria's poems is the same joy as spending time in front of a painting like the El Greco where more and more begins to reveal itself.

Don't miss Gloria's subtle sense of humor; as you read these poems you are being watched. The only two figures in the painting looking directly at the viewer are El Greco himself, in the back row, and his son, in the lower left corner of the painting. When you are at a crowded funeral, to whom are you looking?

Palm Sunday

Always the sky keeps expanding.
Wide as America's brave margins,
wide as my loneliness in the Middle West.
I lean against a dust cloud behind us,
the glory sinking into a muted timberline.
I am drunk with longing. The wind is singing—

my drunken friend, the wind, hurls
sweet curses at my face.
We have learned to love
this road, which lies down like pythons,
refuses to forgive our excesses,
refuses to consider us kin. Our driver's

sign overhead reads, *Jesus is my co-pilot.*
Jesus who crossed the city
gates of his ancestors
on a road carpeted by palms.
Our goodtime driver must know this—
he drives with abandon,

despite our fragile cargo: scholars and accountants,
prophets and exiles all the same to him.
The road, which suggests things, is tired of ceremony.
It lies down to sleep like the snow.
Lie down TallMountain, lie down
Serafin Syquia, lie down Li-Young, lie
down Divakaruni, lie down Eman Lacaba,
lie down pilgrims of the open road.
Shameless, we gather our light
jackets in balls. We rest our heads,

our faces upturned to a squall of stars.
I near the end, my soul recites.

O loneliness, my body responds.
This empty road is a house
where no one lives. What strange fire
we bring when we come to this house.

Goodness

I couldn't contain my hands
from touching the blue and yellow
tiles, the chiseled flourish
of flowers and poems in Arabic
on window frames and doorways
more solemn than a congress of saints.
Such goodness strikes me like panic,
or like the aching beauty
of harelip petals of dogwood blooms.

I remember the two of us young in our bones,
when goodness taught us to sleep side by side,
her waist against mine,
all sea and brine tangled in her hair.

What is it in beauty that renders us helpless?
Awful goodness is what the saints must suffer,
unlike the pleasure we know
when the store clerk gives us change
for a twenty when we handed him only a ten.
Today while folding my shirts and socks
and placing them in cedar drawers
I was suffused with this spell
of goodness as if desire
planted its fist in my solar plexus.

My sister looked after me the way
a lighthouse draws ships to safer harbors.
Faultless as a daylily, a lightness
in her step as if God, who seldom chose unwisely,
had plucked her

roots and petals from His garden.

Last we spoke, my sister,
now some corporate fiscal boss,
was learning me to be
money-wise—sound advice
on aggressive growth mutual funds.
She's mastered the language of deep pockets,
endowments, and the prospect of daily gain.
Money is to her the only measure.

Liquid assets, fat cats in jaunty ascots,
and all the future's other aliases
are nothing more than this bloated present,
of which beauty has no part.
What moved in the dim corridors
I can only say was the spirit of God.
And from there I returned to discover
my waning eyesight,
to squint and filter in the light
of my dislocated origins.

Before desire, goodness was nothing
to Adam and Eve. There were
only the chores in the garden
and God's watchful eye.
And that was it. Nothing.
Goodness calling upon their duties,
their previous lives of nothingness.

Hoodlum Birds

The fearless blackbirds see me again
at the footpath beside the tall grasses
sprouting like unruly morning hair.
They caw and caw like vulgar boys
on street corners making love to girls
with their "hey mama
this" and their "hey mama that."
But this gang of birds is much too slick.
They are my homeys of the air
with their mousse-backed hair and Crayola
black coats like small fry hoods who smoke
and joke about each other's mothers,
virginal sisters, and the sweet arc of revenge.
These birds spurn my uneaten celery sticks,
feckless gestures, ineffective hosannas.
They tag one another, shrill and terrible,
caroling each to each my weekly wages.
But they let me pass, then flit away.
They won't mess with me this time—
they know where I live.

Young Americans

I was eighteen or nineteen when I pumped gas
on the graveyard shift for Standard Oil
at the company station on 19th Avenue and Irving,
a strange intersection of highway and hamlet.
This was after the Arab oil embargo
when gas was rationed, years before I took
Econ 101 and learned the supply and demand axis
and the word anomaly, which I defined for myself.
Pumping gas and washing dishes were not stupid jobs.
Standard Oil supplied me with laundered shirts
shrink-wrapped and pants in hangers, a blue
waist jacket with my name, John, sewn on it.
There are things you can count on as certain
like having your name on your jacket, or Ziggy
Stardust playing, "John, I'm only dancing."
David Bowie turned sixty today and whether
you call it "climate change" or "global warming,"
we are in a new era of geography, unfolding
a new cartography of grease: Young Americans
with Chevrolets and Fords, we had a boss
named Johnny Chan at Standard Oil.
I drove a '68 Mustang with a v8 engine,
black grease caked under my fingernails
and gasoline on my pants that smelled
like fresh paint that never dried.
My friend Duane would die of gunshot wound
in a crossfire between warring Chinese gangs—
Joe Fong's crew and the Wah Chings.
Duane was at the Golden Dragon restaurant
in Chinatown with his girlfriend, coming from a dance.
By 8 A.M. when my shift ended, I had seen the sun creep
up the stunted buildings, the shop doors creaking open,

the *Chronicle* truck dropping off the weekend papers.
I had already heard the dark descanting to the street,
the wail of cop cars crescendo by the time I reached home.
What freedom did I bargain for in sleeplessness?
Was it for pleasure of motion, safe in a car?
Fearlessness I've long outgrown?
"Let there be commerce between us," Clyde
said to the undertaker in *Bonnie and Clyde.*
My one good thesis in college was that
the Barrow Gang was safest in their cars...
Detroit's Big Four was already in trouble.
The exodus from the Motor City began in droves
ten years before my love-in at Standard Oil,
four dozen seasons shy of "Japan Bashings"
and the subsequent murder of Vincent Chin
with a baseball bat, before we named such a thing
as hate crime, before the *Exxon Valdez*
struck Bligh Reef in Prince William Sound,
spilling eleven million gallons of crude oil,
a lake of black as big as the state of Ohio.
Pumping gas in the graveyard shift was
the loneliest job I could find. It was the silence
I bartered for; it was the darkness I knew
the empty highway kept and me illumined
in isolation, catching a glimpse of the ineffable.
David Bowie turned sixty today and I can see
Alan Lau beginning his shift at 8:00 A.M.
Alan who was more anomaly than I shuffled to work
on foot still a little sleepy. The harbors where
we dock our dreams were continents apart,
but there we were trading shifts at Johnny Chan's
gas station—in league with the invisible.

Allegory of the Laundromat

Another Emilie Loring romance, her third in one month:
> *How could she hope that his love would remain*
> *steadfast when he learned her shameful secret?*

It was 1967 and the phenomenal world tethered on the brink
of laundry baskets and record snowfall in Chicago, astronauts
     burning
in their space capsule, Wole Soyinka being hauled to jail

on trumped up charges, 82 arrests in a police raid at a blind pig
in Detroit precipitating a riot. "Here Comes the Night"
was what my sister heard the band rehearsing

on the rooftop three backyards away through a cloisonné
of clotheslines and pulleys. The hippie drummer waved
his drumsticks, my sister wishing for a Van Morrison song.

This was the year Che was ambushed,
the summer Fidel would seek refuge in Spanish Harlem
and pluck chickens on a neighbor's porch stoop, the year

my sister was almost raped at a Laundromat in the Haight.
It was Saturday in fog-banked San Francisco, my sister,
negotiating between delicates and cotton, between dark socks

and semi-dark socks with danger and romance.
There was no escaping that Magdelenic task of laundry,
loads upon nuanced loads she carted from our flat.

She was indentured not to nuns who took in troubled teens
from "good families," but to a mother at work on a weekend.

"When a Man Loves a Woman" played on a scratched 45

over and over from the tomboy's bedroom below our flat.
There was no escaping the oily man in a brown derby jacket
in that near-empty Laundromat that afternoon.

He came from behind and put his left hand across her mouth
and his other on her crotch just when she was about to read
Emilie Loring describe the waywardness of the heart

to the rhythm of the rinse cycle. "Here Comes the Night"
was not playing in her head, but the drummer
walked in on them and spooked her attacker.

The hippie drummer with his dopey Labrador
was on his way to the park...Vietnam, the Six Day War,
black riots in Newark and Detroit, all that bedlam and rage

and it was hotter than an immolating monk in July.
Who cares about the flood of runaways from Nebraska?
Who cares about the indelicate balance of our weekly wash?

Motet

The husband hears *lagrima y fortuna*
        from the fortune-teller reading his palm.

Having asked the wrong questions,
        his sentence is to live here the rest of his life.

The wife nurses a nosebleed.
        She's a tall drink of water.

The wife kisses his neck,
        blood petals on his collar.

Nowhere else can a man imagine the rain
        in his hands, or conspire on white sheets

with the rain whispering
        sweet talk in Spanish.

Boarding the next bus,
        one foot on the sidewalk,

the husband mistakes happiness
        for a loosened apron, a pear

ripening on the sill,
        his wife's hair tucked behind an ear.

The Idea of North

And what did you expect to see
        when you climbed up the stairs
to their bedroom only to discover
        your not-yet-old parents asleep
with the television on?

It has nothing to do with sadness
        when you wake and hear crows cawing
in the eerie trees, their gnarly branches
        like your unruly black hair in the wind.

The idea of north means to risk
        not coming back to what you've left behind,
to know the hour when the quiet window darkens,

        and the blue house disappears with the light.
You've learned to love the smooth bark of birches,
        the circle of trees outside. They must know
that you are nothing without them.

        You come back to that boy
standing in a room of two sleepers,
        their faces illuminated
by the television flicker; and what color

grief must be when you
        stand in the open,
vastly alone, blue August sky behind you.

Ruin

My beautiful, unlucky brother is a deadbeat,
a scofflaw, a veteran of foreign wars.
When the Vietcong god sent him back to us,
my mother prayed to the Virgin
in repentance for her threat to disown him
when he considered Canada instead of the draft.
In Khe Sanh my brother bivouacked through rice paddies,
though I picture him in rubber slippers
along rice terraces in the Ifugao,
in villages beneath a corrugated sky.
When darkness shut into the dark,
he spied the enemy through his nightscope,
marching like a trail of black ants,
loaded down with light
mortars, scant provisions, and their wounded.

After his tour,
I found a snapshot I wasn't supposed to see—
a captive boy, his ankles held up
by a smiling soldier while another is slicing off his balls.
When my brother had arrived at his manhood,
he called me. It was after the neighborhood boys
gathered before Goteng, a part-time
healer and collector of discarded glass.
Circumcised, my brother, slumped on his bed,
his cock wrapped in guava leaf, and bleeding.
In his hand was a gift, the blue marble,
the one he named the *Conqueror.*

Once there was a bridge
that sagged to the river and beckoned him

to drown with all his gear.
And all the women he had ever loved
would take up his bags and bless his failures,
unpack his last clean shirts—white
like his mestizo skin and delicate as his sisters'.

Beautiful, unlucky brother,
sleepwalking amid the ruins, I call
you back to your desires
along the rim of terraces, back
to the shallow water flourishing with young rice.

Palawan

In Sabang an outrigger ferried us
to the leeward side of the island.
A boatman waited to carry us inside

the cave where you hear only the asthmatic
breathing of the gas lamp and the oar's
steady clap against the underground water.

Interior river leading to an interior sea,
Palawan, island of lepers and refugees,
island of dogs and bird-nest poachers.

Palawan, an island in the South China Sea,
where a man with a knife wound lay
in a state of mute grace—his body half-

abandoned, half-redeemed by a woman
combing sweat from his hair
in our jeepney clouded with dust.

Her man's story begins and ends with blood.
His knife, his pride, this idiot thing
he flails like a drunk fumbling for his keys—

a fish vendor posing like a street-corner thug.
Not touching, we lay on our narrow bed.
It was the first night of my wife's menstrual flow,

blood passing through her in slow rivulets.
The simple terrors we invent, the names we give
for our fears: Dalkiel, prince of dogs,

Aziel, lord of knives, this room, our darkest night.
I will betray my wife, and one day she will leave.
When the moon waxes yellow, there is no balm

strong enough to soothe a lover's wound.
The howling of dogs suddenly stopped,
our room now silent, except for the oar

beneath that cave we dreamed of for weeks
with cathedral-tall rocks like deformed wax statues.
In a few hours it would be sunrise.

But we would've already awakened, our packs
and satchels ready. The only jeepney out
would leave at five for Puerto Princesa.

Over unpaved roads we soldier the long ride,
our driver is a terrible angel who hums a bad tune.
A woman sleeps, her face pressed against the smell of rust.

Aubade

Because grief straggles like a bottom dweller
And seldom comes up for air,
He slides one hand through a jacket sleeve

And slings pole and fishing gear in his trunk.
Grief is a basement thing—
A bad mix like drinking and driving if

One is young and openhearted. He drives
His car to the Sacramento Delta. The air
Frigid, the odor of human salt reeks

From his chest. His hands so cold
They could barely hook the worm at the end
Of his line. He lions in the morning,

Sucking breath into breath with his last pack
Of smokes. The inland heat still asleep
In the ground. Nothing but a low moan,

A humming song rises up from a well
Inside his wasted self.
It had no lyrics, this chorus about waiting

In Puccini's opera where a woman full of hope
Peers through a hole pinprick size
To see the harbor lights drag in

The ship that would bring home her beloved.
There are no words for the sun's arrival
Except that it is begotten by song,

A fire spark flickering Pentecostal,
A nascent thing, immigrant and lonely.
Morning begets the honking of geese

The way birds and light beget his happiness
For a father, whom he recalls impeccably
Dressed for his daily departure,

And how the father would pause to hum
His affections, and bless him
With the bread from the oven of his heart.

Blue Miles

Miles Davis is a barbiturate ride of non-sequiturs: blue lines criss-crossing a subway map of Tokyo. When I was ten, all the slickers dripping in the cloakroom were yellow. A girl, one of the Mary Anns or Mary Catherines, had red rubber boots. My father wore a blue Ban-Lon shirt. I kept a blue marble in my pocket. Once I watched my father berated by his boss when I dropped him off at work. Pity the boss for his inconvenience; pity the father if you must for having a son who trashed his car. In my twenties, I heard Miles Davis blow his horn; his back was turned to the audience. This was a couple of years before he died. I was not old enough to understand his horn's conceit, or that

Miles Davis was an idea. "So What" began as a memory of his father. Then two cops came and busted his head open while he was taking a cigarette break outside the recording studio. Copping an attitude is a sure invitation for an ass-whuppin'. In front of a giant sequoia you learn to let go of your conceit. There is snow on the ground like remnants of an accident. In his holy writ, William Matthews proclaims: "Here it comes, Grief's beautiful blow job."

> Someone give my old man a sobriquet
> for his sense of timing, his miscues.
> Someone make him a song
> immediate and transparent!
> Let it be sung with trumpets—
> trouble's durable democracies.

Apple

My people are never the same in memory.
They are the dead come back for a picnic,
a table set with plates of sliced apples.
I am there somewhere hidden in a tree.
In my luckless twenties, still raw from heart-
break and prone to constant hard-ons, I watched
through an open window a woman, middle-aged,
naked, except for her utilitarian bra and panties.
Her hair, teased like a hive of cotton candy,
eyelids, a heavy purple coat. I could almost
smell her—vivid as my first kiss: Maile L.
who had in her mouth some cinnamon Red Hots.
The woman's lipstick was thick like car wax
red and cheap in a dime store way.
She was fitting to go to work at some diner.
I was then a college intern for the lame duck
from my district. I was eager for everything
I imagined this woman could teach me.
This was in the city of Cain where we kept
the doors unlocked for alien thoughts to enter.
If she were the first woman, would that make
me the snake? See, the snake in the garden
was a real smoothie with a killer pickup line.
Me, I was just a salamander on a leaf.
This, before I learned my left from my right,
Rilke from Roethke, Keats from Yeats.
And many more years followed when I didn't
understand a thing completely. Memory
is another name for ghosts and their awful hunger.

Brian Turner

Brian Turner served for seven years in the U.S. Army; was an infantry team leader for a year in Iraq beginning November 2003, with the 3rd Stryker Brigade Combat Team, 2nd Infantry Division. Of course we want to know what really goes on in Iraq, our mainstream media certainly doesn't tell us. (How quickly we forget the U.N.'s covering of Picasso's antiwar masterpiece "Guernica" when Colin Powell made his case to bomb Iraq in February 2003. Maureen Down, in *The New York Times,* said, "Mr. Powell can't very well seduce the world into bombing Iraq surrounded on camera by shrieking and mutilated women, men, children, bulls and horses.") We also need to know the human and cultural aspects that only an artist can communicate. After the "fall of Baghdad" the U.S. military posted Army patrols outside the National Ministry of Oil but did nothing to protect the hospitals, libraries and museums. Turner says, "I wanted to learn as much as possible about the people of Iraq, their culture, their history. I wanted to know more of the history layered into the earth." So it is wonderful that we have Brian Turner's poems because history should not be political. "History is a cloudy mirror made of dirt / and bone and ruin." Stanley Kunitz says, "If we want to know what it felt like to be alive at any given moment in the long odyssey of the race, it is to poetry we must turn." There is a deep sense of pain and loss in these poems that could never be documented any other way. "All of these poems [are] an attempt to remember and to record the personal and the historical I was experiencing while in Iraq," Turner says, "So, even though I often wrote poems of pessimism and poems which investigate pain and loss, I share them because I'm hoping to be a small part of our country's larger meditation on war."

Mihrab

They say the Garden of Eden blossomed here
long ago, and this is all that remains,
wind scorpions and dust, crow-like jays
cawing their raspy throats in memory
of a song, a ghost of beauty
lingering in the shadow's fall.

Let me lie here and dream of a better life.
Let what beauty there is be lifted up
and given to the greater world
as I listen to the mouths of termites
eating of the earth, their bodies
drumming a rhythm in the soil, undaunted
in their blindness, by the millions
raising a skylined architecture
the blood moon must recognize with light.
Let me stay here with these birds
and listen to their rough songs.

If I say the desert is an afterimage,
that birds serenade us, that the moon
is the heart of God shining in heaven,
that if there is a heaven it is
so deep within us we are overgrown,
that the day brings only a stripping of leaves
and by sundown we are exhausted,
then let it be, because if there is a definition
in the absence of light,
and if a ghost can wander amazed
through the days of its life, then it is me,
here in the Garden of Eden,

where it is impossible to let go
of what we love and what we've lost,
here, where the breath of God is our own.

Here, Bullet

If a body is what you want,
then here is bone and gristle and flesh.
Here is the clavicle-snapped wish,
the aorta's opened valves, the leap
thought makes at the synaptic gap.
Here is the adrenaline rush you crave,
that inexorable flight, that insane puncture
into heat and blood. And I dare you to finish
what you've started. Because here, Bullet,
here is where I complete the word you bring
hissing through the air, here is where I moan
the barrel's cold esophagus, triggering
my tongue's explosives for the rifling I have
inside of me, each twist of the round
spun deeper, because here, Bullet,
here is where the world ends, every time.

Alhazen of Basra

If I could travel a thousand years back
to August 1004, to a small tent
where Alhazen has fallen asleep among books
about sunsets, shadows, and light itself,
I wouldn't ask whether light travels in a straight line,
or what governs the laws of refraction, or how
he discovered the bridgework of analytical geometry;
I would ask about the light within us,
what shines in the mind's great repository
of dream, and whether he's studied the deep shadows
daylight brings, how light defines us.

Gilgamesh, in Fossil Relief

It is the month of Ab, late summer
of the seventh century B.C.E., a poet
chisels text into stone tablets, etching
three thousand lines and brushing them by hand,
the dust blown off with a whispered breath.

He is translating the old Sumerian epic,
reinventing the city of Uruk, the Wild Man
and the woman sent out to seduce him.
It is an old story now. It was an old story then,
full of gods and beasts and the inevitable
points of no return each age must learn.

In the mid-August heat of the year 2004,
an archaeologist pauses over an outline
of bone, one body's signature in the earth,
which he reads carefully with a camelhair brush
and patience, each hairline fracture revealing.

History is a cloudy mirror made of dirt
and bone and ruin. And love? Loss?
These are the questions we must answer
by war and famine and pestilence, and again
by touch and kiss, because each age must learn
This is the path of the sun's journey by night.

For Sin-lege-unninni

Observation Post #71

Balad, Iraq

Owls rest in the vines of wild grapes.
Eucalyptus trees shimmer.
And from the minaret, a voice.

Each life has its moment. The sunflowers
lift their faces toward dawn
as milk cows bellow in a field of trash.

I have seen him in the shadows.
I have watched him in the circle of light
my rifle brings to me. His song
hums in the wings of sand flies.
My mind has become very clear.

R&R

The curve of her hip where I'd lay my head,
that's what I'm thinking of now, her fingers
gone slow through my hair on a blue day
ten thousand miles off in the future somewhere,
where the beer is so cold it sweats in your hand,
cool as her kissing you with crushed ice,
her tongue wet with blackberry and melon.

That's what I'm thinking of now.
Because I'm all out of adrenaline,
all out of smoking incendiaries.

Somewhere deep in the landscape of the brain,
under the skull's blue curving dome—
that's where I am now, swaying
in a hammock by the water's edge
as soldiers laugh and play volleyball
just down the beach, while others tan
and talk with the nurses who bring pills
to help them sleep. And if this is crazy,
then let this be my sanatorium,
let the doctors walk among us here
marking their charts as they will.

I have a lover with hair that falls
like autumn leaves on my skin.
Water that rolls in smooth and cool
as anesthesia. Birds that carry
all my bullets into the barrel of the sun.

A Soldier's Arabic

*This is a strange new kind of war where you learn
just as much as you are able to believe.*
                                    —Ernest Hemingway

The word for love, *habib*, is written from right
to left, starting where we would end it
and ending where we might begin.

Where we would end a war
another might take as a beginning,
or as an echo of history, recited again.

Speak the word for death, *maut*,
and you will hear the cursives of the wind
driven into the veil of the unknown.

This is a language made of blood.
It is made of sand, and time.
To be spoken, it must be earned.

Curfew

The wrong is not in the religion;
The wrong is in us.
                            —Saier T.

At dusk, bats fly out by the hundreds.
Water snakes glide in the ponding basins
behind the rubbled palaces. The mosques
call their faithful in, welcoming
the moonlight as prayer.

Today, policemen sunbathed on traffic islands
and children helped their mothers
string clothes to the line, a slight breeze
filling them with heat.

There were no bombs, no panic in the streets.
Sgt. Gutierrez didn't comfort an injured man
who cupped pieces of his friend's brain
in his hands; instead, today,
white birds rose from the Tigris.

In the Leupold Scope

With a 40x60mm spotting scope
I traverse the Halabjah skyline,
scanning rooftops two thousand meters out
to find a woman in sparkling green, standing
among antennas and satellite dishes,
hanging laundry on an invisible line.

She is dressing the dead, clothing them
as they wait in silence, the pigeons circling
as fumestacks billow a noxious black smoke.
She is welcoming them back to the dry earth,
giving them dresses in tangerine and teal,
woven cotton shirts dyed blue.

She waits for them to lean forward
into the breeze, for the wind's breath
to return the bodies they once had,
women with breasts swollen by milk,
men with shepherd-thin bodies, children
running hard into the horizon's curving lens.

Guarding the Bomber

With his legs gone, bandaged at mid-femur,
he palms the invisible above him like a conductor
in difficult passages of light, fluorescent and streaming,
two gauze-wrapped stumps directing movement
from his shoulders as I wipe salt from his lips
with a wet rag, checking the feeding tube, the I.V.
in his neck, listening to his morphined Arabic
as I imagine him lying there in the debris
and settling dust, his brain snapping back
into momentary consciousness, realizing
that his own feet—still in their sandals—
wait for him across the room, and that his hands—
driven beyond the body—negotiate
black wires and hot wires still, arming
explosives in a 155mm shell casing,
much of his body unable to sweat, working here
beyond me and my thoughts of his Paradise,
wondering if the virgins will care for him
as I do, changing his bedpan, bathing him
with sponges and reassurances in English—
a language he hates, its vowels
a smooth sheen of oil on steel—no,
he's far beyond my rifle and desert fatigues,
his ghost limbs dextrous and agile,
and whether I want to admit it or not
he's tending the fire, the explosives
continuing around him, his arms
elbow-deep in the blue flame
and heat, reaching down to touch me.

Ashbah

The ghosts of American soldiers
wander the streets of Balad by night,

unsure of their way home, exhausted,
the desert wind blowing trash
down the narrow alleys as a voice

sounds from the minaret, a soulful call
reminding them how alone they are,

how lost. And the Iraqi dead,
they watch in silence from rooftops
as date palms line the shore in silhouette,

leaning toward Mecca when the dawn wind blows.

Wading Out

—*Ad Duluiyah, Iraq*

We're crossing an open field, sweating in December's heat,
with 1st Squad covering from the brush to our left;
I could be shot dead by a sniper, easily—
this could be the ground where I bleed out in 90 seconds,
but it won't be. There's a patch of still water
I'm about to walk into as I always do,
too much adrenaline and momentum in my stride,
boots sinking ankle-deep and still I slog forward,
M-4 held up over my head. Fiorillo sinks to his knees
to my right—then backs up, makes it out
of the septic runoff I'm up to my thighs in,
the stench filling my nostrils, and it's funny enough
once the mission's done, *Turner running in to swim,*
but no one's laughing anymore, the months turning
into years gone by and still I'm down there slogging
shoulder-deep into the shit, my old platoon
with another year of bullets and mortars and missions
dragging them further in, my lieutenant so far down
I can't reach him anymore, my squad leader hunting
for souls that would mark him and drag him under
completely, better than any bottle of whiskey.
And I keep telling myself that if I walk far enough
or long enough someday I'll come out the other side.
But will Jax and Bosch and my lieutenant make it, too?
If one day we find ourselves poolside in California,
the day as bright as this one, how will we hose ourselves off
to remove the stench, standing around a barbeque
talking football—how?

After Bruce Weigl

Joshua Poteat

Joshua Poteat honors something we often tend to ignore, and that is grief. This section begins, "To live at all is to grieve." Through a series of meditations, nocturnes, and illustrations he looks to the natural world. But Poteat is not a "nature" poet who tends to dwell in abstractions and generalities. He descends *into* the earth, the world of night, "under the cobblestones...[where] even the street lamps have forgotten [him]." This is what Mary Oliver calls "the wound of being alive." Poteat understands that perhaps we should try for a little more reverence and a little less worship. His is an "inner voice," as Oliver notes, "flowing forward, throwing out its lovely perceptions, its lyrical lines of praise, its wonderment, its pursuit of moments and places, past and present, where mystery's veil for a moment sparks upward." But, she continues, these out flowing words are "suggestive of more than simple thought, darker than pensive, deeper than reflective. [They are] closely associated with devotion."

Nocturne: For the Doves

On the side of a desert road
                                a headless dove,
            its body a basket of ants,
                        basket of creosote stems.

To live at all is to grieve
                                and from what life
            did we gain this trust,
                        awake each dawn

to find the bright air
                                full again,
            rustle and coo
                        in the widening palms?

Nocturne: For the Aviaries

Then the rain came,
       full of a sadness I've never seen before,
through the cottonwoods
       and along the river,
which is no longer a river
          but an apparition under the sand.

Had I five hummingbirds,
       I would make a love charm
and string them from the tongue
       of a small copper bell in those branches,
          necks hovered together, broken.

Had I a swan, it would sleep
       under the hives
with a bucket of fresh milk,
          with the splintered white faces of goats.

To reclaim or take apart the night,
       like the city does, carving through
the blind river?
          The brilliant debris of stars, the air?

Nothing in this world is ours.

Illustrating the theory of ebb and flow
[Plate 6, Fig. 23]

When I have had enough of reason

      I turn to the evening boughs

among the wild fern,
           steam on the horse's back,

the tidy white guts of ants spread

      across the floors, and field after field

of fireflies saying *I'm here,*
         make love to me, I'm here.

Every bit of it simple, entire, intact,

      maybe even ordinary.

All the essential lonelinesses
      giving account of themselves.

Grass Meditation

i. Deer in the Grass

Ghost, come closer.
　　　　—T. Roethke

It is better to have nothing,
for at last even our bones will fall.
I tell you this, deer,
because you die so well,
and yet, transcendence aside,
press the tips of the moving grass
with an indifference made for men,
for the wind tonguing the frost.
Here we are, deer. Get up.
Tell us how to live.
Even the rim of gnats reeling
your honeycombed brain want to know.
I once thought that nothing
could ever die. Walking through
these suburbs at twilight,
front lawns glowing,
each sprinklers' Morse code
a pattern that could save us all,
a sweet clatter of bats in the cherry trees...
who could leave a place like this?
Deer, come closer. Ignore the ruin.
You won't be loved through
the long rains. Remember the foxes
wading the river, so alive in their dusk,

in their murderous little worlds.
I watched you live a life among the grasses:
your small bone feet,
your toes all fallen like petals.

ii. Common Names of Dune Grass (Festuca Mollis)

Pintongue, repose, sandhair, sweet
thumbs, angel bed, pillow grass, lissome.
To go from disorder to order
in moments with the glorious naming:
that voice, pure in the mind's wide,
gasping easement…that paraffin
of Latinless joy, twilight bats
feeding on fireflies.
What gave us the mouth to hold
the water of these nights?
What gave us the wound?
Some would say the soul,
but the docks in the distance,
and even the mud under them,
are filled with a light
I cannot seem to find in the living.
And the sea, indolent, fish-eyed,
washes the hooves of wild horses,
scarred from barnacle and clam.
It is this that wounds, that brings us
to our knees: the solitude of a foal
sleeping under the shore pines,

the warmth of its breath…starry campion…
wild pea…is all we could ever want.
So *Festuca Mollis*, keep it to yourself.
I'll name the ghosts alone tonight,
because the earth, goddamnit,
the earth provides.

iii. *The Suffering of Grass*

is not suffering at all.
It is of itself, and does nothing
but sway, the wind a way to touch,
finally, after a hundred mornings of silence.
In his journals, Petrarch asked himself,
Don't you think grass deserves better?
It was Petrarch who also said, *Life never finishes,*
after meeting Siamese twins in a monastery,
their bone hearts torqued together,
their hands fluttering like doves.
Early in his own life he refused to love
any child, wincing at every little foot
in his front yard. It was the grass he loved,
and determined, through the sweet rot
of cuttings, that it does feel,
and thus suffers, mostly.
Anything that rots, suffers.
If we must go, let it be by flame.
If we must go, let this earth grow
to grass again. Or not.

Lying here in my neighbor's
perfect viridian expanse,
I admit to feeling nothing,
even though just last week,
a mockingbird in the shriveled
longleaf pine sang the first eight notes
to *You and the Night and the Music,*
and I sighed at the sound,
thinking of Petrarch asleep
on the lawns of his youth,
so fed up and devious, never knowing
that the way to the earth's vastness is not
through the front yards
or the suffering of grass,
but to be sure we remain whole and pale
in the sky of our one true life.

Illustrating the illustrators

[See Plate 123, Fig. 16-17]

When we wrote the name that we were told

      was ours, the name that contained all

we would be given and all that would be lost,
         there was a pleasure in the small, exact

movements of our hands, the pencil a machine,

      worshipped, and that was where it began.

We said *Let us be children together,*
         and we drew our lives before the body.

We drew the coal-quay whores with wooden legs,

      the tow-horses asleep against the fog. Even dusk

flooded a whole new darkness, a sympathetic ink.
         We said *If death is like this then give us more.*

Illustrating the destroyers

[See Plate 172, Figs. 31 36]

When the larvae hatched in the birches,

  all black and hunger and ruinous,

the leaves emptied themselves
    and gave us branches so clean

the caterpillars grew, clinging through

  the rains. There was the give and pull

of air in the tent nests, there was the tug
    of kerosene in the remains.

A new kind of evening began,

  a leafless warmth in the trees,

the bark was alive and we did
    what we could to keep the world ours.

Illustrating that objects on earth
can throw shadows into space
[Plate 27, Fig. 6]

The cows rested in the shade, white cows,

      all born for the rack, and I walked around them,

a nod hello, across the hidden meadow to a place
          where nothing grows.

Devil's stomping ground it was called.

      God help us if the ground gives us up.

What devil isn't made of earth, though, of red bark
          and steam, and the winters of our past where ice

gathered in the trees, each glistening rail a small blade

      to slip under a toenail at sunset. With awe comes necessity,

and through the hills, I felt a thickening, a loss, and I could not
          see what the night would do without us.

Illustrating the chinquapin oak
[Plate unknown]

Repeat: *if the leaf is canoe shaped, with a short stem,*

      it is chestnut. If the leaf is thick and pale beneath,

with a slender stem, it is chinquapin oak.
      It is a quiet mistake to make.

Look for the pale side above the wind.

      From the hills it will look like snow returning.

Walk towards the oak with gnats in your ears,
      with the rabbits startled from the bush.

There will be movement in the low branches.

      Small wings and the river's open mouth.

The dirt rising in every bloom.
      The grouse-light of regret.

You will recall a day like this, sudden, immense

      at your throat, and what.it is to live, and to have lived.

Illustrating

I see fireflies as logarithm, the meadow

     as paper tacked to the charcoaled morning.

I blame only myself. I'm drawn to the misfortune
        of others, so here is my place, my apple-tree chair,

and hope comes and goes like daylight

     on the flatlands road to which we have been condemned.

As a child, I would mock death and recline in the fields,
        ants mating in my hair, hoping that a vulture

would mistake me for carrion. (Now *that's* living.)

     I flooded my pants in goat's milk, faked entrails

of rope and wine and leeches. I believed
        the vulture's wing would touch my face

and cure me of this life, that its eyes

     would reveal the secret way to dying, never aware

that we had invented each other, bird and I,
        bone and voice. I know there are better ways

to suffer, and I found them later, all the names for light

     used up and shredded, thrown to the cellar mice.

It runs in the family, this nonsense of death.
        My father was born with a knife in his mouth.

My mother was a great, reddened moon fit for harvest,

    and like all beautiful creatures, she had to consume herself.

What I want from God isn't theorem, isn't formula, isn't blueprint,
        isn't sight, isn't prescription, isn't medicine, isn't
            ghost, isn't.

Apparatus to show the amount
of dew on trees and shrubs
[Plate 23, Fig. 36]

Go to where memory will come again:

      Summer under the insolvent orchard.

The timothy grass coned long for cows
             and the one-eared lamb, blue-flies dead

in troughs. Under the orchard where

      the rotting pears, those dull sparks

in the grass, could warm a man's hands
             with wasp sting, with the sap of a love

elegant and sweet, willow's catkin in the briar.

      Forgive the pastoral. It can do nothing

but bring us back to wherever it is
             we came from, each branch tempered

with a dew grown bitter across the leaves,

      and here I sit, an old man among the pears, the wasps,

the beautiful shape of a lamb falling towards me.
             If I say this moment I am living through

is being lived for the first time by me, I am wrong.

The earth is not lost, not dear.

I know it will not take me back.
    I have not lived enough to earn this yet.

MAURICE MANNING

Bucolics, Maurice Manning's third book, and one of the most beautiful books to come along in years, is a collection of psalms meditating on the reciprocal relationship between the divine and the human, the creator and the created. It opens with an epigraph from George Herbert, "Shepherds are honest people, let them sing." What is most haunting about these poems is that behind this honest and direct connection the speaker has with his creator is the knowledge that we have pretty much destroyed our earth, our inner lives, and therefore our connection with God. Galway Kinnell says, "The more we conquer nature, the more nature becomes our enemy, and since we are, like it or not, creatures of nature, the more we make an enemy of the very life within us."

Manning's second book, *A Companion for Owls,* consists of poems in the voice of Daniel Boone. In "Eight Analytical Questions" Manning/Boone asks,

> Why do I dream of crows winking like black eyes across
>   the sky?
> Who discovered salt? What is the source of two objects
> against each other: a bug against a leaf,
> the leaf against a bed of moss, the moss
> against the earth, the earth against the womb
> the moon has made from circling the earth, the womb
> against the boundless sea of heaven?

One reviewer says, "This is somewhat ridiculous and preposterous.... Boone lacked an extensive formal education.... Manning's Boone, on the other hand, writes complex, magniloquent 'Meditations.'" This would be why most biographical and "persona" poems, which are wildly popular among poets today, fail. But Manning is not afraid to let his self show through the character of

Boone. It's like putting a mask on so that the true self can still be heard. Manning speaks through Boone in order to ask the questions that might otherwise be self-consciously stilted. Kinnell also says, "...for the poem to be interesting, the persona would have to represent a central facet of the poet's self."

Opposition to Bridges

If a man cannot cross a river on its own terms,
then he doesn't deserve the other side. If he
is loathe to feel pulled down or set adrift,
or so cold his lungs refuse to take in air,
he's afraid to be a human waterwheel;
a river doesn't care if we agree
with its course or the fact of its flow. The same is true
for trees: we must go with their grain or else
they break—all thresholds and wagon hubs and flint-
lock rifle stocks depend on one direction,
which I call straight. Cold science has it wrong:
it is a body waiting and not at rest—
the root desire to move—that moves a man;
a bridge will take away the meaning of
the river and deny the love of crossing.
This is how to cross a river: strip,
and breathe, then feel the current in your bones;
forget that drowning is a word and sink.

On God

Is there a god of the gulf between a man
and a horse? A god who hovers above the trench
of difference? Not a god who makes us notice;
but a god who rakes his hand through the air and makes
a space neither can enter. What about
a god of animal innards? Some god
whose sole creation cleans the blood of an elk?
Perhaps there's a god of petty disaster
who breaks wagon wheels and paints clouds across
an old man's eyes. Consider the gods of flint
and primer who work side by side with the gods
of spark and steel; then there's the god of aim
and the god of near death—a god commonly praised.
Consider a god of small spaces, a fat
man's misery god, who lives in the shadow
between two rocks and sleeps on moss, content
with the smallness of his task; the god who bends
rivers, the god who flecks the breast of a hawk,
the god who plunders saltworks. I once thought
one god looked over my shoulder and measured
my steps, but now I believe that god is outnumbered
and I am surrounded by countless naked gods,
like spores or dust or birds or trees on fire,
the song, the grit, the mean seed of nakedness.

Eight Analytical Questions

Who decides the shape of rocks,
the curl of cedar branches, the ripples
wrinkled down a bedrock stream?
Why do I dream of crows winking like black eyes across the sky?
Who discovered salt? What is the source of two objects
against each other: a bug against a leaf,
the leaf against a bed of moss, the moss
against the earth, the earth against the womb
the moon has made from circling the earth, the womb
against the boundless sea of heaven? Who
decreed when spring should start? Whose task is it
to grant the rain permission to fall and feed
the rivers? Who draws rings around the hearts of trees?
Upon my soul, I wonder who invented beauty?

On the Limits of Natural Law

I draw in breath. My legs move.
My head turns, my eyes narrow.
My hand takes hold of a buckeye branch
and strips it of its leaves. The world
is all around me. The world reaches
to me like a wife. I put my weight
against it, my bones belong to it.
My heart is full of ether,
the air beyond the sky.
It cannot be touched, I cannot
lay it in the dirt. This conflict
is older than all the rivers.
How many miles are all
the rivers put together?
My legs will never know.
But my heart does;
and it is not a distance.
It is similar with birds:
the reason that they fly
has nothing to do with wings.

Bucolics [I]

boss of the grassy green
boss of the silver puddle
how happy is my lot
to tend the green to catch
the water when it rains
to do the doing Boss
the way the sun wakes up
the leaves they yawn a bit
each day a little more
for a tiny reason then
when the leaves outgrow their green
the wind unwinds them Boss
that's the way you go around
if you loose me like a leaf
if you unburden me
if I untaste the taste
of being bossed by you
don't boss me down to dust
may I become a flower
when my blossom Boss is full
boss a bee to my blue lips
that one drop of my bloom
would softly drop into
your sweetness once again
if I go round that way
I'll know the doing means
to you what it means to me
a word before all words

Bucolics [XLVII]

I put my face against
the horse's shoulder Boss
I breathed into the frost
so white upon his coat
I saw the patch I left
a darker spot as dark
as darkness gets I let
the horse cut through the field
the spot was looking out
an empty eye unblinking
unblinking Boss which one
of us was that supposed
to be O was it you
so steady Boss or was
that patch of empty me

Bucolics [LIX]

when I see the shadow of the hawk
but not the hawk itself do you know
what it feels like Boss a stone a stone
set on my chest it weighs me down
it's stronger than the horse's strain
against the plow lines Boss it's like
the river after rain I can't
hold back the pull the pull that makes
me like its heft I even like
the shadow's tiny yoke O Boss
I feel its curve around my neck
I see a flap of wings so black
it binds me to the furrows Boss
a shadow smarter than the sting
of a switch though it is lighter than
a feather though it is thinner than
a leaf that shadow stone is one
of many wonders Boss for all
the world it makes me think of you
you heavy thing you never move

Bucolics [LXXII]

you leave a little night inside
the flower Boss to keep it closed
although the sun is up above
the middle branches of the tree
the flower has a little night
inside it I can see it Boss
a drop of pitch a pinch of sleep
as if the flower wants the night
to last a little longer than
it does I'm like the flower Boss
sometimes I want the night to last
so I can keep on sleeping when
I'm sleeping I don't have to think
about you Boss it's harder than
a summer field that hasn't seen
the rain for days to think about
you Boss do you know that you stone
you're hard to get around you're like
the morning always there when my
eyes flutter open when they see
the daylight coming softly that's
a laugh a thing so hard it starts
out easy Boss when I wake up
I feel a feather on my face

Bucolics [LXXVI]

thank you for the leaf Boss
thank you for the tree thank
you for the knife-edge wind
thank you for the breath behind
the wind breath sweeter than
a horse's sweet oat breath
thank you Boss O thank you
for the yellow-belly sun for
the moon fatter than a tick
thank you for the season
thank you for the long-leg
shadows Boss thank you
for paring down the day
today for bossing all of it
away except the fish-eye sky
O except the leaf that leapt
into my hands thank you for
two hands to make a cup
to hold the leaf Boss thank you
for the red bug riding on the leaf

Old-Time Preachin'
on a Scripture Taken from a Tree

A mind unhitched to a heart?—Shuckies!
if a mind don't drag a heart behind it

like a pony cart, I say, what kind
of mind is that, but wandered off,

and not just astray, a-lost! That heart
is like a tree cut from its roots—

a sip of freedom, spiked with the gall
of death, a breathing in without

the chance to let it go. That's what
a theory is, my friends, 'taint real,

it's rootless and unrooted in time,
and also meaning. Yes, to mean

means not just now, but all the way
to yonder. A good idea is good

because it begs a spell to reach.
Now, a tree will not deny its roots

and roots will not betray the ground
they're woven to, and none of it

will say there's no such thing as sun
or wind or rain.—That makes a heap

of hearts hitched up to trees. Now ask
yourself which is more free, a tree

or you, and which of the two gives freely?
By grabbies, what's true for trees is true

for mountains, rivers, birds—gracious!
this is where you're livin' and everything

you love is here! Now ain't that
a pleasant breeze, and ain't that

a lovely rustle in the leaves?
To hear it is to hear ourselves

belonging where we live, and blessed.
But let's not think together we

have found this perty thing; let's know
it is the other way around:

we're found and made and rooted here,
and bound to being where we're bound.

I hope we're going to the heart,
I hope we're tied up in that glory.

O, recall that hilltop sermon and all
those blessings flowing from it for

the meek and poor, them other folks

half-whipped. If you can see where such

a river winds right down to you—
you salt and pepper of this earth—

then look up and pinch your eyes to see
just where that river got its start:

you'd best believe that mount is real
and where we always are forever.

Let us think about that with our hearts,
beating in amen time. Amen.

The Lord He Thought He'd Make a Man

You know dem bones are gonna rise—
no doubt about it, even the bones

of a bad man rise, even the bones
of your own voice singing rise,

though it's easy to think they won't. They lay
unsung for years and then one day

you're all grown up with a pack of sorrows
and you start humming something strange,

and it all makes sense, the coming back
of the past and what we're calling bones—

and there's bones aplenty. Remember the song
about the fox and the chilly night?

Well, he goes out alright and what's
he got when he comes back? A goose,

and pretty soon he's cooked it up
and the little ones are suckin' on

the bones-o, bones-o. Remember what
Aunt Rodie's waiting for? The death

of her old gray goose so she can get
a good night's sleep. That's two dead geese

by my count and it just gets worse. When she—

whoever the hell she is—comes round

the mountain, all the folks will be
so glad, they'll kill the old red rooster.

She must have been a prodigal
of sorts. It doesn't matter where

she's been or where she got the money
to buy those six white horses, nope,

she's coming back and everything
will be right as rain when she comes round.

Unless you're the rooster. It hurt to sing
the song back then; you wanted to save

that rooster and put him in the barnyard
of another song, and now, when those bones

have come back red and sad, it hurts
again and maybe more, because

you see your life has been one sorrow
after another and still you love it

like a child who knows no better. You want
your bones to rise but only if

you get to take the sorrow, too.
Now why is that? Because there is

another song you used to sing.
This man gives his love a cherry without

a stone, and a chicken without a bone
and a story that never ends, and a baby

who never cries. It's what they call
a riddle song. It riddled all

the others because it was happy
and sad at once. It seemed to be

a song about another place,
the place where you were born and raised

the first go round, and when you rise
again you hope it happens there.

Ars Poetica Shaggy and Brown

Tell me the story in your heart.
Does it involve a donkey? Does

the donkey have a name? I know
a donkey whose name is Clyde. I like

Ole Clyde. When I walk to the patch
of cedars on the hill, I whistle,

and Clyde comes up from the barn he likes
to wait in. What's a-goin' on?

I say, then Clyde swishes his tail
and looks me in the eye. I nod,

he nods, then both of us cock our ears
and look around. We wait and wait.

Most of the time there's nothing to hear,
nothing to notice, but a hawk

riding the last hot swell of the day
or a spider spinning. Well, tally-ho,

I say in a little while. He swishes
his tail again—Lord, I believe,

help thou my unbelief. Well, now,
he doesn't come out and say it, but that's

what he means by that easy swish. It looks

like a by-God moment to me. Maybe

you'd like to put Ole Clyde in the story
in your heart; it would be alright, I guess.

Ole Clyde has seen it all. He saw
the old man hang himself in the barn.

He saw the rope the old man carried,
and watched the milk can topple over.

The old man gave one kick and that
was it. Well, there I go! I've put death

and God together again! Now all
I need is love. I guess it's there;

it always is, according to Clyde.
Right now, above my head I count

eleven dragonflies. You know
some people call them skeeterhawks?

You reckon I could ever run out
of stories in my heart to tell?

Chris Abani

At the age of eighteen, Nigerian poet and novelist Chris Abani was imprisoned following the publication of his first novel and was released six months later. When his second novel, *Sirocco*, was published in 1987, government forces seized it and Abani was again arrested, detained at Kiri-Kiri Maximum Prison (also known as Kalakuta Republic) and accused of sedition. In 1991 he was arrested for the third time, again taken to Kiri-Kiri, and held on death row, tortured by electric shock, and held for six months in solitary confinement. He knows what is at stake. As Terrance Hayes puts it, his poems are "made of fire." Natasha Tretheway tells us that through poems like "Aphasia" Abani "reminds us that even as we live in a time of lost language—of meaningless sound bites and empty slogans—it is the poet's job to find words that can, as Keats puts it, sharpen one's vision into the heart and nature of man." But Abani points out that we should be careful not to define him by his experiences. In an interview with Carlye Archibeque Abani says, "The art is never about what you write about. The art is about how you write about what you write about." He goes on to say,

> Artists were essentially shamans or priests or seers in the old days and I think art is still the primary focus of looking for ways to deal with the questions of being human. I think you can do that while meditating in your room. OK so I went to prison, I suffered, but I'm here drinking a three-dollar coffee checking my email on a fancy gadget. The problem is we're looking for something that doesn't exist. We're looking for authenticity. There is no such thing as authenticity. There is either good art or bad art. Art is never about its content it's always about its scaffolding.

In *Uses of Enchantment*, Bruno Bettelheim says, "In order not to be at the mercy of the vagaries of life, one must develop one's inner resources, so that one's emotions, imagination, and intellect mutually support and enrich one another." But he leaves out one of the most crucial elements, the body. In "The New Religion" Abani says, "The body is savage."

> But this distance I keep is not divine,
> for what was Christ if not God's desire
> to smell his own armpit?

Prelude

There is a story—I cannot tell it.

> Remembering is not always good.

This is not my story—I shouldn't tell it—these cannot be my words.

> Still:
> A stranger is a better judge of fairness between twins.

This is everybody's story—we must tell it.

> And.
> Shame is finding ourselves in the details.

Om

1.

The hills of my childhood are purple with dusk and wings—
guinea fowl launched like a prayer to the still forming moon.
I hold Bean's shell to my ear. There is no sea. But only sea.
By my bed, in an empty chair, my shirt unwinds.
I remember my aunt counting the dead in the newspaper.
I never told anyone that every sliver of orange I ate
was preceded by words from high mass.
Peramea secula seculurum.
Spit out pit. Amen.
Juice. Amen. Flesh.

2.

A full moon leaning on a skyscraper. The taste:
qat and sweets on a tropical afternoon.
The dog's black tongue was more terrifying that its teeth.
The gravestone rising out of the puddle was more sinister
than the body we discovered as children swinging
in the summer hot orchard.

3.

The old woman singing a dirge has a voice of dust.
Sorrow lodged like a splintered bullet next to the heart.
A man once asked me in the street:
Do you own your own bones?
She likes the home I come in, I say to Cristina

as we drive towards the Golden Gate.
Bean, I repeat.
She loves the home I come in
and I am alive with fire and scars.
Here is my body, I say, eat it, do this,
Remember me—

4.

Even now melancholy is a skin flayed
and worn in dance through the city.
Yes, the city becomes skin too and wears me
as skin and I want to say; this is my body, as I stroke
the curve of the fountain in the park.
This is my blood. Drink it. Remember.
The safety of doorways is an illusion.
They lead nowhere.
This is why we build houses.
Sand, when there is no water can ablute,
washing grain by grain even the hardest stone of sin.
But you, but you, you are a sin that I live for.
Ne Me Quitte Pas. Ne Me Quitte Pas. Ne Me Quitte Pas.
Nina Simone's voice walks in dragging bodies,
dead black men that bled unseen in the dark
of Southern nights, shaded by leaves
and the veiled eyes of hate.
And in a poem, Lucille stands in the shadow of a tree
and pours libations for our souls,
for our salt, for our gospel.

5.

Somewhere a man speaks
in the dark, voice lost to rain.
I know this hunger, this need
to make patterns, to build meaning
from detritus; also the light
and the wood floor bare but for the lone slipper
tossed carelessly to one side. I admit the lies I've told.
Look, nothing has been true
since that picture of hell on the living room wall lost its terror.
I say I want a strong woman, but unlike Neto
I cannot have the woman and the fish.
The war followed.
Children are losing their souls to the heat.
That is to say, poor American soldiers.
The rich have found a way to charge theirs to Amex.
Ask this: what is the relationship of desire to memory?
Here is a boy in the airport café, hair cropped from service.
And he closes his eyes to take a sip of coffee.
And smiles as the dark washes the desert away.

6.

Los Angeles:
A red sky and angels thick like palm trees,
and garbage blown in the wind like cars
and the gluttony of SUV's
in an endless river of traffic.
Through the dark, we say, through the dark:

but do we ever really know?
There is a man in a field and he is searching for God.
Father, he says, father.
In the distance, birds, traffic and children.
There is a blue sky. There is a sky blue with night.
The call of the earth is a primitive song,
stomping feet and broken men.
There is a blue sky. And night.
The city is a flock of lights.
The darkness of tunnels like caves is knowledge,
also mortal. Maps are like God.
They are the city yet not the city.
They contain the city but yet do not.
We trace the lines in loss.
Sometimes we find treasure.
Sometimes something fills the mind,
something at which we pause, stopped.
The way a photograph cannot remember the living.

7.

To die is to return.
To fly is to be a bird's heart.
Neither is freedom.
If it were we would have no name for it.
No language. Not even the temptation of wind
blowing a dark woman's hair away from a cliff's edge.
Instead, feathers are brought to my door everyday by mystery.
Kindling for a fire, a beacon, an epiphany I cannot light.
This is the body of Christ.
Santificum.

Sacrament

I.

Have you heard of the oracle of the Igbo?
The one called Chukwu? Just one word: God.
The oracle of God.
The voice of God.
The final arbitration.
Kpom kwem.
Deep in a grove of trees, the sacred lake,
and rising in the gloom and heat,
mist, the very breath of divinity.
The unbearable trepidation,
the worship, the sheer terror and earnestness
trembling the supplicants. And the priests
sitting on rocks and in trees on haunches,
silent like vultures or Rilke's unspeakable angels.
And then a pilgrim wades cautiously into the lake.
On the shore, the line of unannointed
shivers in a shared awe.
And if the petitioner is beautiful or strong,
the priests hold them under, then shackled,
for slavers. In the lake, red dye bubbles up
as God smacks his lips.
And that endless line of believers near faint
with the fearsome beauty of the thought:
Please eat me too, God.
Eat me and find me worthy.
But don't let me die.

2.

There is risk in this—
Not the words, but the dreaded embodiment of light,
a sacred song. A river darker
than caverns immeasurable,
a sacred river; not all ganga, not all alf,
but still fire, still fire.
Before this flight, before this persistence
the soul is bare.
Holy the water.
Holy the smoke.
Holy the flame.
Holy, holy, holy.

3.

Death is a flock of blackbirds low over muddy streets
in war torn Sarajevo. Dirt stained walls yearn
for all that is night. Elegies fall like raw silk.
If there is a way it is here.
Salt and ash.
This is how the Igbo clean their teeth.
Grandmother grinding charcoal
coughing as the silt rises.
Then salt rubbed into the black
as though morning were trying to temper night.
Then water and a fingertip collecting the gray,
the unidentifiable finger dipping into
a mouth held open like a wound—

A thick sludge fills my conscience.
It is made of the dissolved bones and flesh
of men we buried in swamps
behind the wall of internment. Buried
in shallow graves like a hand cupped in peat,
then bodies and lime: the hiss and sizzle, and the suck
of earth filling with water.
Of swamp digesting histories and love.
Instead of a preface, instead of a requiem,
the symphony of rain fills the night
with the distracted hurry of wild horses
crossing a plateau under a threatening sky.
I am not afraid of love, or its consequence of light,
Joy intones, chant like skin, like sand, like water.

4.

There is fog this morning. On my continent
children die. African children die every day.
It's what they do.
I can still hear my mother's sewing machine
stitching the afternoon with promise. Under a tree,
in the scent of rotting fruit, I washed
bitter-leaf for dinner. Washed and squeezed.
The bitter foaming away.
Like frothy green blood from the neck of sacrifice.
A dog is barking at spirits in the heat.
Language escapes me still—see it sprinting
down the street. Crazed. A crazy man.
Babbling. Babel. This is my language.

On a wall in Sarajevo, graffiti reads:
KILLING IS MY BUSINESS
BUSINESS IS GOOD. THE FROGMAN.
Sem gave me the book with the graffiti.
In DC he said, my name is Sem,
eyes narrowed, even as his lips smiled.
I know this trim. A name for invisibility.
A loss for a chance to be here.
Do I not carry a pocketful of accents?
In halting speech I said it wrong: Semezdin Mehmedinovic.
He smiled as though I were singing an aria.
We went back to coffee, the dark, and rain:
a Washington DC street and the glow of lights.
Agi Mishol said, choose your rabbe carefully.
Someone who sees who you can become.
I doubt there is anything like truth here in this teashop
but the chai is good and the light on Bean is golden.

Muir Woods

In this Cathedral Grove, trees rise in devotion
older than words. In the red-tinted light
stands a woman in a black yashmak. Only her
eyes are visible and they lock onto a black-tailed deer,
its red coat fanning through the green. Her hands fly
to her mouth to contain the rush, but the words are out.
Every man turns toward the delicate husk; her voice.
And her husband's face betrays the knowledge.
This is how God unstitches our fear.

Dark Waters (III):

Born from a flower

        Its face darkens the world

    To be forgotten

            The gazelle's leap before the snare

Who broke the string for me?

The New Religion

The body is a nation I have not known.
The pure joy of air: the moment between leaping
from a cliff into the wall of blue below. Like that.
Or to feel the rub of tired lungs against skin-
covered bone, like a hand against the rough of bark.
Like that. "The body is a savage," I said.
For years I said that: the body is a savage.
As if this safety of the mind were virtue
not cowardice. For years I have snubbed
the dark rub of it, said, "I am better, Lord,
I am better," but sometimes, in an unguarded
moment of sun, I remember the cowdung-scent
of my childhood skin thick with dirt and sweat
and the screaming grass.
But this distance I keep is not divine,
for what was Christ if not God's desire
to smell his own armpit? And when I
see him, I know he will smile,
fingers glued to his nose, and say, "Next time
I will send you down as a dog
to taste this pure hunger."

The Old Artist Speaks to the Young Poet

Each visitation changes something.
Let the angel go and climb the ladder.
There is God in this effort. This thing
is more existential, only not desire.
To the left, metal assemblage leans lazily
into rust. He runs arthritic hands
over its rough. You always work
with something, he says. This is
an actual horse's leg. Nicely weathered.
Why if it weren't for the nails it would run away
with the picture. Chagall would like that.
A blank television regards me—
The news and the weather, he says.
With time, he says, everything dissolves into art

Say Something about Child's Play

The soldier asks the boy: Choose which
do I cleave? Your right arm or left?
The boy, ten, maybe nine, says: Neither,
or when I play, like a bird with a broken wing
I will smudge the line of the hopscotch
square, let the darkness in.

The soldier asks again: Choose which
do I cleave? Your right leg or left?
Older in this moment than his dead father, the boy
says: Neither, or when I dance the spirit dance,
I will stumble, kick sand in the face of light.

This boy says: Take my right eye,
it has seen too much, but leave me the left,
I will need it to see God.

Acknowledgments

Ruth Forman

"Stand," "Koi," and "Classified #7" From: *Prayers Like Shoes* (Whit Press, Seattle, WA) by Ruth Forman. Copyright © 2008 by Ruth Forman. Reprinted with permissions of the author and publisher.

"If You Write Poetry, Graduate School," "Hand Me Your Palm," "Let It Heal," "Healer," "The Journey," "We Walk," "Kin," and "Risk" reprinted from *Renaissance*, published by Beacon Press. © 1997 by Ruth Forman.

Ilya Kaminsky

"Stranger" first appeared in *Gulf Coast.*

"Of Deafness" first appeared in *Image.*

"A Toast" first appeared in *Harvard Review.*

"That Map of Bone and Opened Valves" first appeared in *Kenyon Review.*

"Author's Prayer," "Dancing in Odessa," "Envoi," "Paul Celan," "Elegy for Joseph Brodsky," "Marina Tsvetaeva," and "My Mother's Tango" reprinted from *Dancing in Odessa*, published by Tupelo Press. © 2004 by Ilya Kaminsky.

Malena Mörling

"Never Mind," and "A Father to His Son" appear here for the first time.

"A Story," "Happiness," "An Entrance," "In the Yellow Head of a Tulip," "Maps," "My Shadow Falls Out of My Body," and "If There Is Another World" reprinted from *Astoria*, published by University of Pittsburgh Press. © 2006 by Malena Mörling

"Visiting," "In a Motel Room at Dawn," and "Standing on the Earth Among the Cows" reprinted from *Ocean Avenue*, published by New Issues Press. © 1999 by Malena Mörling.

Kevin Goodan

"How the Soil Dampens for the Loss of Thee" and "We Pass and They Pass and the World Abides" appear here for the first time.

"Theories of Implication," "Near the Heart of Happening," "Between Brightness and Weight," "If I'm Not a Garden," "Gearing Housed in Twilight," "Losing Something Important," "Saudade," "Snow Angels," "August," and "In Chesaw Falling Behind" reprinted from *In the Ghost-House Acquainted*, published by Alice James Books. © 2004 by Kevin Goodan.

Jay Leeming

"Two Months After" appears here for the first time.
"Rowboat," "Apple," "Organ Music," "I Want to Go Back," "Law Office,"
"Supermarket Historians," "The Light Above Cities," "She Killed the Spider,"
"I Pick Up a Hitchhiker," "Grandpa Putting Salt on His Ice Cream," and "Song
of the Poison in the Executioner's Needle" reprinted from *Dynamite on a China
Plate*, published by The Backwaters Press. © 2006 by Joseph M. Leeming.

Terrance Hayes

"Cocktails with Orpheus," "Mystic Bounce," and "Stick Elegy" first appeared
in *Poetry*.
"Clarinet" first appeared in *Isn't It Romantic: 100 Love Poems by Younger American Poets*,
published by Verse Press.
"Wind in a Box," "Talk," "The Blue Etheridge," "The Blue Terrance," "Wind in
a Box (I want to always sleep...)," "Wind in a Box (Even the dirt dreams...),"
"Wind in a Box (I claim in the last hour...)," and "Threshold" reprinted from
Wind in a Box, published by Penguin. © 2006 by Terrance Hayes.

Luljeta Lleshanaku

"Waiting for a Poem," "Child of Nature," "Monday in Seven Days" and "The
Mystery of Prayers" appear here for the first time.
"Memory, And the Sun is Extinguished, More than a Retrospective, Sunday
Bells, The Bed, Out of Boredom, and "Nocturne. Soft Whistle" reprinted from
Fresco, published by New Directions. © 2001 by Luljeta Lleshanaku.

Sherwin Bitsui

"Calyx" and "Flood Song" first appeared in *To Topos Poetry International*.
"Atlas," "Blankets of Bark," "River," "At Deer Springs," "Red Light," "Bullet
Wet Earth," "The Sun Rises and I Think of Your Bruised Larynx," "Bodies
Wanting Wood," "The Four Directions of a Lie," and "Trickster" reprinted
from *Shapeshift*, published by The University of Arizona Press. © 2003 by
Sherwin Bitsui.

Maria Melendez

"Love Song for a War God," "An Ocean of Code," "Knot of Prayer," and "Ann's
Answer" appear here for the first time.
"Remedio," "Tonacacihuatl: Lady of Our Flesh," "Between Water and Song,"
"Backcountry, Emigrant Gap," "Why Not Attempt the Summit," and "An
Argument for the Brilliance of All Things" reprinted from *How Long She'll Last in
This World*, published by The University of Arizona Press. © 2006 by Maria
Melendez.

Translations

Luljeta Lleshanaku

"Memory" translated by Henry Israeli and Albana Lleshanaku.
"Waiting for a Poem," "Child of Nature," "Monday in Seven Days," and "The Mystery of Prayers" translated by Shpresa Qatipi and Henry Israeli.
"And the Sun is Extinguished" translated by Henry Israeli and Lluka Qafoku.
"More than a Retrospective" translated by Henry Israeli and Ukzenel Buçpapa.
"Sunday Bells" translated by Henry Israeli and Alban Kupi.
"The Bed" translated by Henry Israeli and Albana Lleshanaku.
"Out of Boredom" translated by Henry Israeli and Qazim Sheme.
"Nocturne. Soft Whistle" translated by Henry Israeli and Luljeta Lleshanaku.

Valzhyna Mort

"Teacher," "Was it a hair you lost…," "A Poem about White Apples," "Juveniles," "Fall in Tampa," and "Belarusian I" translated by Valzhyna Mort with Elizabeth Oehlkers Wright and Franz Wright.

BIOGRAPHIES

RUTH FORMAN is an acclaimed poet and former teacher in June Jordan's Poetry for the People program at UC Berkeley. She is the author of three award-winning books: poetry collections *We Are The Young Magicians* (Beacon, 1993), and *Renaissance* (Beacon, 1997), and a children's book, *Young Cornrows Callin Out the Moon* (Children's Book Press, 2007). Her latest poetry collection is *Prayers Like Shoes* (Whit Press, 2009). Her work is widely anthologized. Ruth is the recipient of The Barnard New Women Poets Prize, The Pen Oakland Josephine Miles Literary Award, The Durfee Artist Fellowship, the National Council of Teachers of English Notable Book Award, and recognition by The American Library Association. She teaches and provides readings and workshops nationally and internationally to a wide variety of audiences and has presented in forums such as the PBS series *The United States of Poetry* and National Public Radio. Also a graduate of the USC School of Cinema-Television, she collaborates often on music, dance, theatre, and media projects. Ruth has taught at the University of Southern California and the Antioch University MFA in Creative Writing program. She is also a nine-year faculty member with the VONA-Voices Workshop.

ILYA KAMINSKY was born in Odessa, former Soviet Union in 1977, and arrived in the United States in 1993, when his family were granted asylum by the American government. He is the author of *Dancing in Odessa* (Tupelo Press, 2004), which won the Whiting Writer's Award, the American Academy of Arts and Letters' Metcalf Award, the Dorset Prize, and the Ruth Lilly Fellowship given annually by *Poetry* magazine. In 2008, Kaminsky was awarded Lannan Foundation's Literary Fellowship. Currently, he teaches in the Master of Fine Arts Program in Creative Writing at San Diego State University.

MALENA MÖRLING was born in Stockholm in 1965 and grew up in southern Sweden. She is the author of two books of poetry: *Ocean Avenue* which won the New Issues Press Poetry Prize in 1998 and *Astoria* published by Pittsburgh Press in 2006. She has translated poems by the Swedish poet Tomas Tranströmer, a selection of which appeared in the collection *For the Living and the Dead*, published by Ecco Press. She was awarded The Rona Jaffe Foundation Writers Award in 1999 and in 2004 the Lotos Club Foundation Prize. In 2007 she was awarded a John Simon Guggenheim Foundation Fellowship. She is currently editing *Swedish Writers On Writing*, forthcoming from Trinity University Press. She is currently Assistant Professor in the Department of Creative Writing at The University of North Carolina, Wilmington and Core Faculty in The Low Residency MFA program at New England College.

KEVIN GOODAN was raised on the Flathead Indian Reservation in western Montana and worked for many years fighting forest fires. His first book, *In the Ghost-House Acquainted* (Alice James), received the L.L Winship/PEN New England award, and his second book, *Winter Tenor* (Alice James), was published in 2009.

JAY LEEMING is the author of *Dynamite on a China Plate*, a book of poems published by The Backwaters Press. His poems have appeared in a variety of magazines including *Ploughshares, The Gettysburg Review, Poetry East* and *Black Warrior Review.* He has been a featured reader at Butler University, the Omega Institute, Robert Bly's Great Mother Conference and the Woodstock Poetry Festival, and is the recipient of a Creative Writing Fellowship from the National Endowment for the Arts. He lives and teaches in Ithaca, New York.

TERRANCE HAYES is the author of *Wind in a Box* (Penguin 2006), *Hip Logic* (Penguin 2002) and *Muscular Music* (Carnegie Mellon University Contemporary Classics, 2005 and Tia Chucha Press, 1999). His honors include a Whiting Writers Award, the Kate Tufts

Discovery Award, a National Poetry Series award, a Pushcart Prize, three Best American Poetry selections, and a National Endowment for the Arts Fellowship. His poems have appeared in a range of journals, including *The New Yorker, Poetry, The American Poetry Review,* and *Ploughshares.* He is a Professor of Creative Writing at Carnegie Mellon University and lives in Pittsburgh, Pennsylvania, with his family.

LULJETA LLESHANAKU was born in Albania. She is the author of six collections of poems in her language: *Femijet e Natyres, Palca e Verdhe, Antipastorale, Gjysem-kubizem, Kembanat e se djeles,* and *Syte e somnambules.* She is also the author of a book in Italian language *Antipastorale* (LietoColle 2006, Italy) and a selected book of poems *Fresco* published by New Directions 2002. Her poems are published also in *Grand Street, Iowa Review, Quarterly West, Seneca Review, New Letters, Modern Poetry in Translation* and in anthologies such as World Beat-*International Poetry Now* (New Directions 2006). She graduated for Literature in the Tirana University in Albania and in 1999 she was a fellow of International Program of Writers, Iowa University. She is the winner of "Silver Pen 2000" national prize. Lleshanaku was the 2008-09 International Women's Forum Fellow at Black Mountain Institute, University of Nevada.

SHERWIN BITSUI is originally from the Navajo Reservation in Arizona. He currently lives in Tucson, Arizona. He is Diné of the Todich'ii'nii (Bitter Water Clan), born for the Tl'izilani (Many Goats Clan). He holds an AFA in Creative Writing from the Institute of American Indian Arts. He is the recipient of the 2000-2001 Individual Poet Grant from the Witter Bynner Foundation for Poetry, the 1999 Truman Capote Creative Writing Fellowship, a Lannan Foundation Marfa Writers' Residency, a 2006 Whiting Writers' Award and, more recently, a 2008 Tucson Local Genius Award. His books are *Flood Song* (Copper Canyon Press, 2009) and *Shapeshift* (University of Arizona Press, 2003).

Maria Melendez has published three collections of poetry: the chapbook *Base Pairs* (Swan Scythe Press, 2001) and *How Long She'll Last in This World* (University of Arizona Press, 2006), which received Honorable Mention at the 2007 International Latino Book Awards and was named a finalist for the 2007 PEN Center USA Literary Awards. *Flexible Bones,* her third collection of poetry, was published by the University of Arizona Press in 2010. She co-coordinates Poetas y Pintores: Artists Conversing with Verse, a traveling exhibition of contemporary Latino art and poetry. She lives in Pueblo, Clorado, and is Editor/Publisher for *Pilgrimage* magazine.

Valzhyna Mort was born in Minsk, Belarus. Her first collection of poems *I'm as Thin as Your Eyelashes* came out in 2005. Mort made her American debut in 2008 with a poetry collection *Factory of Tears* (Copper Canyon Press), co-translated by the husband-and-wife team of Elizabeth Oehlkers Wright and Pultizer Prize-winning poet Franz Wright. She is the recipient of Crystal of Vilenica award in Slovenia in 2005 and Burda Poetry Prize in Germany in 2008. She has received fellowships from the Polish Ministry of Culture and Literarisches Colloquium Berlin, Germany. She currently lives in Washington D.C. and teaches part-time at the University of Baltimore.

Eugene Gloria's second collection of poems, *Hoodlum Birds* was published by Penguin Books in 2006. His recent poems have appeared or are forthcoming in *Lake Effect, The Normal School, Louisville Review,* and *The New Republic.* He is a recipient of the Asian American Literary Award and a Pushcart Prize. He teaches creative writing and literature at DePauw University and lives in Greencastle, Indiana.

Brian Turner is the author of *Here, Bullet* (Alice James Books, 2005; Bloodaxe Books, 2007). He has recently completed a second collection, *Phantom Noise,* which will be available from Alice James Books in early 2010. His work has appeared in *The Georgia Review, The Virginia Quarterly Review, Poetry Daily,* and the *Crab Orchard Review,* among others. He has received an NEA Fellowship in Poetry and a Fellowship from the Lannan Foundation. He currently lives in California and is working on his third collection of poetry.

JOSHUA POTEAT's books include *Meditations* (Poetry Society of America National Chapbook Prize, 2004), *Ornithologies* (Anhinga Press Poetry Prize, 2006), and *Illustrating the Machine that Makes the World* (University of Georgia/VQR, 2009). Over the last few years he has won prizes from *American Literary Review, Bellingham Review, Columbia, Marlboro Review, Nebraska Review, River City, Hunger Mountain,* and many others. Recently, poems have appeared in *Virginia Quarterly Review, Blackbird, Indiana Review, American Letters & Commentary, Ninth Letter, Handsome, Copper Nickel* and others. Born in Hampstead, NC, Joshua lives in Richmond, VA, where he works as an editor of assorted texts.

MAURICE MANNING's most recent book of poetry, *The Common Man,* is forthcoming from Houghton Mifflin Harcourt. Manning is from Kentucky, where he lives part of the year. He teaches at Indiana University and in the MFA Program for Writers at Warren Wilson College.

CHRIS ABANI's prose includes *Song For Night* (Akashic, 2007), *The Virgin of Flames* (Penguin, 2007), *Becoming Abigail* (Akashic, 2006), *GraceLand* (FSG, 2004), and *Masters of the Board* (Delta, 1985). His poetry collections are *Hands Washing Water* (Copper Canyon, 2006), *Dog Woman* (Red Hen, 2004), *Daphne's Lot* (Red Hen, 2003), and *Kalakuta Republic* (Saqi, 2001). He is a Professor at the University of California, Riverside and the recipient of the PEN USA Freedom-to-Write Award, the Prince Claus Award, a Lannan Literary Fellowship, a California Book Award, a Hurston/Wright Legacy Award, a PEN Beyond the Margins Award & the PEN Hemingway Book Prize.

NORMAN MINNICK (editor) was born in Louisville, Kentucky. His collection of poems, *To Taste the Water* (Mid-List Press, 2007), won the First Series Award. He received his B.A. in Art and English from Marian University in Indianapolis and was accepted to the creative writing program at Florida International University in Miami. He earned his M.F.A. in 2001 and was awarded an Academy of American Poets Prize that same year. Minnick returned to Indianapolis where he lives with his wife and two young children.